FINALLY IN THE LAND

God Meets His People's Needs

JOHN MACARTHUR

THOMAS NELSON
Since 1798

Published in Nashville, Tennessee, by Thomas Nelson. Thomas Nelson is a trademark of Thomas Nelson, Inc.

Published in association with the literary agency of Wolgemuth & Associates, Inc.

Layout, design, and writing assistance by Gregory C. Benoit Publishing, Old Mystic, CT. $\overset{\text{C}}{\underset{\text{B}}{\text{G}}}$

Thomas Nelson, Inc. titles may be purchased in bulk for educational, business, fund-raising, or sales promotional use. For information, please e-mail SpecialMarkets@ThomasNelson.com.

Scripture quotations are taken from THE NEW KING JAMES VERSION. Copyright © 1982 by Thomas Nelson, Inc. Used by permission. All rights reserved.

ISBN 978-1-4185-3403-5

Printed in the United States of America

10 11 12 13 RRD 5 4 3

Contents

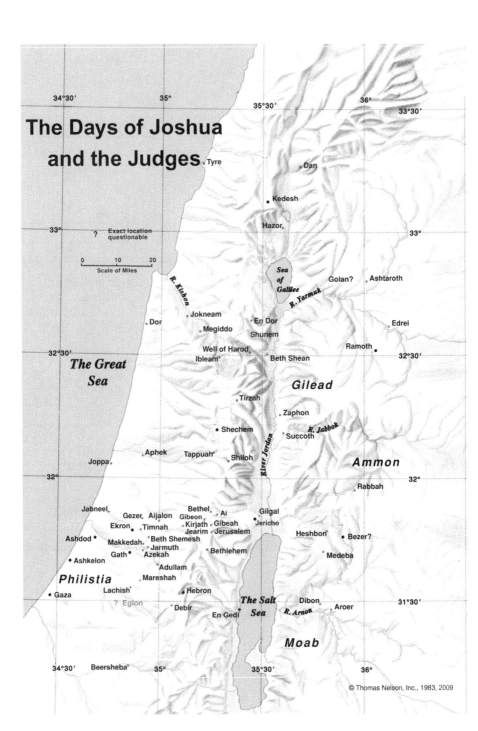

The Days of Joshua
and the Judges

Tyre

Dan

Kedesh

Hazor

? Exact location questionable

0   10   20
Scale of Miles

Sea
of
Galilee

Golan?   Ashtaroth

R. Kishon

R. Yarmuk

Jokneam

Dor

Megiddo

En Dor

Edrei

Shunem

Ramoth

**The Great
Sea**

Well of Harod
Ibleam

Beth Shean

Gilead

Tirzah

Zaphon

Shechem

R. Jabbok

Succoth

Aphek   Tappuah   Shiloh

Joppa

River Jordan

Ammon

Rabbah

Jabneel   Bethel   Ai   Gilgal

Gezer   Aijalon   Gibeon   Jericho

Ekron   Timnah   Gibeah

Kirjath   Jerusalem   Heshbon   Bezer?

Jearim

Ashdod   Beth Shemesh

Makkedah   Jarmuth

Gath   Azekah   Bethlehem   Medeba

Ashkelon   Adullam

Philistia   Mareshah

Lachish   Hebron

Gaza   ? Eglon   The Salt   Dibon   31°30'

Debir   Sea   R. Arnon   Aroer

En Gedi

Moab

Beersheba   35°

© Thomas Nelson, Inc., 1983, 2009

INTRODUCTION

After the Exodus from Egypt (see my study guide titled *Exodus from Egypt: Moses and God's Mercy*), the people of Israel, now freed from slavery, wandered in the wilderness for forty years—but that was not the original plan. The people were supposed to go directly from the land of bondage into the promised land of Canaan, but they had been unwilling to trust God, so He waited until *an entire generation* died before leading the nation of Israel into Canaan.

Our studies open at the time when the Israelites are entering Canaan, under the leadership of Joshua. Beginning with the crossing of the Jordan River, we will cover a span of many hundreds of years, culminating in the life and death of Samson. During this time period, we will discover two overriding themes: (1) God's people lived in a continuing cycle of sin and repentance, but (2) God was *always* faithful.

In these twelve studies, we will examine some of Israel's great battles in Canaan, including the battle of Jericho. We will also study the lives of some of the Bible's heroes of the faith (such as the judges), as well as a few of God's people who failed miserably. As we read, we will jump back and forth in chronological history, looking at one historical period and then skipping forward or backward in time as needed. You will read about twelve spies, a prostitute-turned-rescuer, a stolen wedge of gold, and much more. Through it all, you will learn some precious truths about the character of God, and you will see His great faithfulness in keeping His promises. You will learn, in short, what it means to walk by faith.

ᔰ What We'll Be Studying ᔰ

This study guide is divided into four distinct sections in which we will examine selected Bible passages:

Section 1: History. In this first section, we will focus on the historical setting of our Bible text. These five lessons will give a broad overview of the people, places, and events that are important to this study. They will also provide the background for the next two sections. This is our most purely historical segment, focusing simply on what happened and why.

SECTION 2: CHARACTERS. The four lessons in this section will give us an opportunity to zoom in on the characters from our Scripture passages. Some of these people were introduced in section 1, but in this part of the study guide we will take a much closer look at these personalities. Why did God see fit to include them in His Book in the first place? What made them unique? What can we learn from their lives? In this practical section, we will answer all of these questions and more, as we learn how to live wisely by emulating the wisdom of those who came before us.

SECTION 3: THEMES. Section 3 consists of two lessons in which we will consider some of the broader themes and doctrines touched on in our selected Scripture passages. This is the guide's most abstract portion, wherein we will ponder specific doctrinal and theological questions that are important to the church today. As we ask what these truths mean to us as Christians, we will also look for practical ways to base our lives upon God's truth.

SECTION 4: SUMMARY AND REVIEW. In our final section, we will look back at the principles that we have discovered in the Scriptures throughout this study guide. These will be our "takeaway" principles, those which permeate the Bible passages that we have studied. As always, we will be looking for ways to make these truths a part of our everyday lives.

⊱ ABOUT THE LESSONS ⊰

⊱ Each study begins with an introduction that provides the background for the selected Scripture passages.

⊱ To assist you in your reading, a section of notes—a miniature Bible commentary of sorts—offers both cultural information and additional insights.

⊱ A series of questions is provided to help you dig a bit deeper into the Bible text.

⊱ Overriding principles brought to light by the Bible text will be studied in each lesson. These principles summarize a variety of doctrines and practical truths found throughout the Bible.

⊱ Finally, additional questions will help you mine the deep riches of God's Word and, most importantly, to apply those truths to your own life.

SECTION 1:

HISTORY

In This Section:

～ I ～
CROSSING INTO CANAAN

JOSHUA 3–4

⋏ HISTORICAL BACKGROUND ⋏

A generation prior to this passage, the Lord had led the people of Israel out of Egyptian slavery and into the Sinai desert. (Read Joshua 1 for background on Joshua's commission from the Lord.) There He had revealed Himself to His people in many dramatic and powerful ways. He had given them the Ten Commandments on tablets of stone. He had moved in front of them through the desert in a pillar of cloud by day and fire by night. He had miraculously provided them with food and water; had delivered them from the most powerful army on earth; and had parted the Red Sea before them so they could cross on dry land. God had not only performed many great miracles but also promised the Israelites repeatedly that He would drive out their enemies before their arrival in the land God had promised them—Canaan.

Yet the people had come to the banks of the Jordan River, the last boundary to cross prior to entering Canaan, and had rebelled against God and His servant Moses. The Lord had told them to cross the river—but they had refused to obey Him, wanting instead to return to Egypt. As a result of this rebellion, the Lord decreed that the entire generation of adults aged twenty and older would not enter the promised land. The nation of Israel had then wandered in the wilderness for forty years, until that entire generation had died.

As our study passage opens, Israel has arrived once again at the banks of the Jordan River, and a new generation is preparing to cross into Canaan. Moses has died, and the Lord has appointed a new leader for the people: Moses' former assistant, Joshua. Joshua had been present on that fateful day forty years earlier when the people rebelled. He had urged them then to obey the Lord's command and continue forward into Canaan—and that is the very reason God chose him to succeed Moses.

Now the people are poised to cross the river, and the Lord has told them that He will work a great wonder on their behalf, just as He had done decades earlier for their parents. This time, the people will obey and walk across the riverbed into Canaan, despite the fact that there will be many battles to fight there. Once they cross, the Lord tells them, they are to remember His great faithfulness to them, and to pass the stories of God's faithfulness to future generations. God's people must not forget what the Lord has done for them, as the previous generation did, and they must see to it that their children don't forget it either.

⌒ READING JOSHUA 3:1–17 ⌒

GATHERING AT THE RIVER: *The Israelites are now camped at the banks of the Jordan River, just across from the city of Jericho. They were here once before—some forty years before.*

1. JOSHUA: This story took place shortly after the death of Moses. Joshua had served for many years as Moses' assistant, and he had also been one of twelve men sent into Canaan four decades earlier to spy out the land. On that occasion, ten of the twelve spies brought back a bad report and urged the Israelites to return to Egypt rather than enter the promised land. Only Joshua and Caleb had urged the people to obey God by crossing the Jordan into Canaan, and the Lord had rewarded them by permitting them to enter the promised land—while the rest of their generation had died in the wilderness (Numbers 13–14). Now, as this chapter opens, Joshua, Caleb, and a new generation are preparing to enter Canaan.

3. THE ARK OF THE COVENANT: The ark was a sacred chest that the Lord had commanded the Israelites to build when they first left Egypt. It was an ornate work of art, made of acacia wood, approximately four feet in length and a little more than two feet high and deep. It was surmounted with gorgeous carved angels, and the entire container was overlaid in gold—inside and outside (Exodus 25). The ark contained the tablets of the Ten Commandments, as well as Aaron's rod and other symbols of God's deliverance from Egypt. It was not the ark's contents, however, that made it so sacred to the Israelites; it was the fact that it represented the very presence of God. The carved angels on top of the ark symbolized the mercy seat, the place where God's glorious presence was made manifest to Israel. The ark itself pictured the throne of God.

THE PRIESTS . . . BEARING IT: The ark was supported on two long poles and carried on the shoulders of four priests, one at each end of the poles.

4. THERE SHALL BE A SPACE BETWEEN YOU AND IT: The people of Israel were commanded to stay back roughly one thousand yards from the ark on their journey across the Jordan. (A cubit is approximately eighteen inches.) This was a sign of reverence for the presence of God, as the ark signified that He was with His people. The ark itself was to be treated with care and respect: only priests from the tribe of Levi were permitted to carry it, and no one was allowed to touch it.

THAT YOU MAY KNOW THE WAY: Another reason for staying back from the ark was to permit all the people to see it. Since the ark visually indicated that God was leading the people, He wanted everyone to be able to freely view the symbol of His presence. It was important for the people to remember that they were following God rather than men as they entered new territory, since they had forgotten that fact many times in the past. Whenever God's people forgot that He was in sovereign control of their circumstances, they became afraid and rebelled against His leadership. We tend to do the same today.

SANCTIFY YOURSELVES: *The Lord commands the people to prepare themselves, because they are about to see His power demonstrated in a very dramatic way.*

5. SANCTIFY YOURSELVES: Sinful mankind cannot enter the holy presence of the Lord, so the Israelites were commanded to purify themselves in preparation for moving forward with God's presence. The Lord had provided detailed instructions on how the Israelites were to keep themselves pure, as well as instructions on how to consecrate themselves when something (such as contact with a dead body) had made them ceremonially impure. These rites and procedures, however, were only outward ways of addressing mankind's sinful condition; an animal sacrifice could not fully atone for anyone's sin. Today, Christians are fully forgiven and sanctified on the basis of Christ's once-for-all sacrifice. Even so, we are called, like ancient Israel, to keep our lives pure and to live as consecrated people.

6. CROSS OVER: That is, cross over the Jordan River.

8. STAND IN THE JORDAN: The priests were to take a visible stand in the middle of the Jordan River so that the entire nation could see them. They were the ones chosen to approach the insurmountable barrier that stood between Israel and the promised land, symbolically opening the way for Israel to cross. The Lord Jesus would also stand one day in the Jordan River, to be baptized as He began His earthly ministry (Matthew 3). He was the one who would finally remove the barrier that stood between mankind and God—the barrier of sin—and He would remove it *forever.*

10. DRIVE OUT FROM BEFORE YOU: This reminder was important for the people of Israel, since the last time they had arrived at Jordan's banks, they had listened to bad counsel and become filled with dread of the Canaanites. They determined that they could not defeat the Canaanites—which was true, as far as their own strength was concerned. Yet they had seen the Lord defeat the army of Pharaoh, and He had promised that He would also overcome the people of Canaan. But they did not believe, and their lack of faith had cost an entire generation the opportunity to enter the promised land. Now Joshua reminded their children to not become afraid but instead place their trust in God's power.

16. Adam: Approximately fifteen miles north on the Jordan River. See the map in the Introduction.

the waters . . . were cut off: The Lord had worked a very similar miracle when the Israelites crossed the Red Sea under the leadership of Moses, more than forty years earlier (Exodus 14). The Lord was reiterating for the people that He would remove any obstacle that stood between them and their inheritance in Canaan. He was also showing the Israelites that Joshua was His chosen leader, just as Moses had been previously.

17. all Israel crossed over on dry ground: Once again, the Israelites were able to cross a body of water that moments before had stood as a barrier between them and the promised land—and they crossed without even getting their feet wet, for the Lord had done all the work on their behalf.

⌁ Reading Joshua 4:1–24 ⌁

Set Up a Memorial: *Twelve men—one from each tribe—carry a large stone on their shoulders out of the Jordan riverbed. Those stones will be for a memorial.*

2. twelve men: Moses had sent twelve men, one from each tribe, into Canaan some four decades previously to spy out the land. Ten of those men, however, had returned to the camp with an evil report, telling the Israelites that the land was full of giants and fortified cities, and urging them to return to Egypt rather than enter Canaan. This time, rather than spying out the fortifications of the enemy, the Lord commanded the twelve to set up a memorial to what He had done—and would do—for them. The Lord was teaching His people to focus on His power and faithfulness, not on the obstacles that stood against them.

3. out of the midst of the Jordan: The twelve stones were selected from the bed of the Jordan River, rather than from its banks. This would stand as proof to future generations that Israel had walked across the river on dry ground.

5. a stone on his shoulder: These stones were evidently quite large.

6. when your children ask in time to come: Here the Lord was instructing His people in something very important: how to teach their children about the character of God. This is not the only time He had taught this lesson: "Only take heed to yourself, and diligently keep yourself, lest you forget the things your eyes have seen, and lest they depart from your heart all the days of your life. And teach them to your children and your grandchildren" (Deuteronomy 4:9).

7. THESE STONES SHALL BE FOR A MEMORIAL: The people of Israel had previously demonstrated the ease with which people forget about God's past blessings—particularly when faced with present obstacles. The Lord wants His people to *remember* His faithfulness, His great works of deliverance, His miraculous power—in short, to remember *Him*. For that reason, Jesus instituted a "remembrance feast" just prior to His crucifixion, a memorial we know as the Lord's Supper, or Communion.

THE PEOPLE OBEY: *A generation earlier, the Israelites had refused to obey the Lord's chosen leaders. This time, they willingly submit.*

8. JUST AS JOSHUA COMMANDED: Some forty years previous to this, Joshua had urged the people of Israel to obey God's command to enter the promised land—and the people had rejected his counsel, to the point that they were ready to stone Moses (Numbers 14:10). That entire generation had died, and now the people were prepared to obey the Lord and submit to His appointed leader.

19. THE TENTH DAY OF THE FIRST MONTH: This was the day that the Lord commanded Israel to kill a lamb in preparation for the tenth plague in Egypt; that is, the Passover Lamb (Exodus 12:3). This day of Passover was very important in the Jewish calendar (equating to March/April in our modern calendar), and it was the very day when Christ was crucified.

20. GILGAL: Approximately a mile from Jericho. See the map in the Introduction.

21. WHAT ARE THESE STONES?: The memorial stones served several purposes. They reminded the people of what the Lord had done in their lives, and they also sparked questions from others, such as future children. The Israelites, like Christians today, were responsible not only to remember the Lord's grace but also to instill awe in their children concerning the things of God.

24. ALL THE PEOPLES OF THE EARTH MAY KNOW THE HAND OF THE LORD: Ultimately, the memorials were to serve as a testimony not merely to one's own family but to the entire world. Like Old Testament Israel, the church is to be a testimony of God's goodness, inciting a curiosity in the world around us, a hunger to know more about the God of our salvation.

⌁ First Impressions ⌁

1. *If you had been traveling with the Israelites, how would you have reacted to crossing the Jordan River on dry ground?*

2. *Why did the Lord command the Israelites to pile up twelve stones on the far side of the river? What things can we do, in our lives, to proactively remember the faithfulness of God?*

3. *Why did the Lord command one man from each tribe of Israel to carry a stone? How does this connect with God's commands to teach future generations?*

4. *Why were the Israelites commanded to keep a great distance between themselves and the ark of the covenant?*

⌁ Some Key Principles ⌁

God's people are to remember His faithfulness.

God had performed great miracles in bringing His people out of Egypt, defeating Pharaoh's army, parting the Red Sea, along with many other marvels. What's more, He had vowed time and again that He would lead them safely into the promised land of Canaan. But when the Israelites reached the shores of the Jordan River, they had lost heart and convinced themselves that their enemies were too powerful for them, refusing to cross the river, as God had told them to. As a result of that disobedience, an entire generation died in the wilderness.

For this reason, the Lord commanded the next generation to set up a monument at the banks of the Jordan, so they would never forget what He had done to lead them into the promised land. In the future, when they faced powerful enemies, they could look back at those twelve stones and remember what the Lord had done for them already—and take courage to trust Him for the future as well.

Jesus instituted a similar memorial just before He went to Calvary, commanding His followers to break bread on a regular basis as a way of remembering what He had done to secure our salvation. "And when He had given thanks, He broke [the unleavened bread] and said, 'Take, eat; this is My body which is broken for you; do this in remembrance of Me.' In the same manner He also took the cup after supper, saying, 'This cup is the new covenant in My blood. This do, as often as you drink it, in remembrance of Me.' For as often as you eat this bread and drink this cup, you proclaim the Lord's death till He comes" (1 Corinthians 11:24–26).

It is vital that Christians teach their children the things of God.

The Lord reiterated several times that the memorial stones were to be a sign not just for the people of that generation but for their children and children's children, to all future generations. The monument was intended to provoke questions from curious youngsters and to give parents an opportunity to tell their inquisitive children about all God had done for His people. We will see in future studies, however, that the people of Israel were not faithful in this, and generation after generation departed from the ways of the Lord—because the parents had not effectively taught their children.

"And these words which I command you today shall be in your heart," we read in the book of Deuteronomy. "You shall teach them diligently to your children, and shall talk of them when you sit in your house, when you walk by the way, when you lie down, and when you rise up" (6:6–7). There are many ways parents can teach their children: through words and actions, lifestyle and example, consistency and longevity. All of these elements are integral to teaching children, but another important aspect includes thinking through practical ways to help them regularly remember the Lord's faithfulness. "Train up a child in the way he should go," wrote King Solomon, "and when he is old he will not depart from it" (Proverbs 22:6).

Treat the things of God with reverence.

The Lord commanded the people of Israel to cross the Jordan behind the ark of the covenant, but they were to keep a great distance back from it. This was a sign of deep respect for the ark, which symbolized God's very presence with His people.

Their reverence served another purpose as well: the distance they kept from the ark enabled the entire nation to see it, and it drew the attention of the world around them to the ark, rather than to the people. By remaining a thousand yards back, there could be no doubt that it was the power of God that parted the Jordan River, since the waters divided the instant the priests' feet touched it.

This is actually a corollary to the previous principle: by holding the things of God in deep reverence, parents make it easier to teach their children to do the same. We draw our children's attention to the Lord and His commands by treating Him and His Word with respect, and it becomes easier for children—and for our neighbors—to see the hand of God at work in our lives.

◟ DIGGING DEEPER ◞

5. *What practical things do you and your family do to continually remember God's goodness and faithfulness? What things might you start doing in the future?*

6. Why is it so important to teach children about the things of God? What happens if parents fail in that duty?

7. Why did the Lord command the people to simply pile stones on top of one another, rather than building an ornate shrine? What does this suggest about the focus of our own memorials?

8. How is the Lord's Supper like the memorial that the Israelites built? How does it differ? Why is it important to observe on a regular basis?

9. Do you treat the things of God with suitable reverence? What areas might the Lord be calling you to take more seriously?

10. Are you faithful in teaching others about the things of God? What lessons do your children, neighbors, or coworkers learn from observing your life?

～ 2 ～
THE FALL OF JERICHO

↜ HISTORICAL BACKGROUND ↝

The people of Israel had crossed the Jordan River and were preparing to enter the land of Canaan, which the Lord had promised to give to the descendants of Abraham. However, there were many people already living in Canaan, and the region was peppered with several strong and fortified cities. Taking the land was going to involve warfare, and the Israelites would have to prepare themselves for battle.

The very first city in front of them was Jericho, a very well-fortified town. In Joshua's day, that meant it was surrounded with solid, massive walls made of mud brick and stone. These walls were often several feet thick, and many cities—including Jericho—had two such walls, with a space between. The only way to enter such fortifications was through the main gate, and those gates were as strong and well guarded as the walls themselves.

Jericho itself was built on a tall mound of land, surrounded by an earthen embankment. It boasted a protection of two bulwarks, one inside the other. The outer wall was six feet thick, the inner one twelve feet thick. Nothing is specifically known of its gate system, but it probably consisted of two gates, one in each wall, with a stone or brick tunnel connecting them. To attack the city, an enemy would have to charge uphill, climb over the embankment, and attempt to breach both gates—all while being shot at from above.

How were the Israelites to take such a city? They were not a trained army, and they had no high-tech weaponry at their disposal. What they did have, however, was more than enough: the presence of almighty God! As the people stood gazing upon this powerful city, it must have become clear to them that the battle belonged to God, not to them.

A Visit from the Lord: *Joshua has a face-to-face encounter with God Himself, very similar to the calling of Moses at the burning bush.*

5:13. Jericho: See the map in the Introduction. Jericho was built atop a hill a few miles west of the Jordan River. The city was fortified by a double ring of walls—a combined eighteen feet thick. Timbers were laid across the top to connect the two walls, and houses were built there. (The prostitute Rahab, whom we will meet in Study 6, lived in one of these houses.)

A Man: This was the Lord Himself in a pre-incarnate appearance (called a *theophany*) as the Angel of the Lord. The naked sword in His hand indicated that He had come to exercise judgment—in this case, against Jericho.

14. as Commander of the army of the Lord I have now come: The Lord was about to bring about a great victory for His people, but it would not be through the military might of the Israelites—it would be through "the army of the Lord." He would perform the great victory so that the glory would be His alone. Again, the Lord made it clear that this particular visit was for the purpose of judgment. (The Lord had once appeared to Abraham, as well, in like manner. He had visited Abraham at his tent, sharing His plans with him, as one friend to another.)

fell on his face to the earth: Joshua had not realized at first whom he was addressing, probably only being startled with the powerful and majestic appearance of the Man. As soon as he realized that he was in the presence of the Lord, however, he threw himself facedown on the ground and worshipped. He also dramatically changed the tenor of his questions from "Whose side are You on?" to "How can I serve You?"

15. Take your sandal off your foot: This was an outward demonstration of humility and respect. Moses was given the same order to remove his shoes when the Lord called him into service as leader of His people (Exodus 3).

Closed for the Day: *The people of Jericho have heard about the Lord's great miracle at the Jordan River, and they are terrified of Israel.*

6:1. securely shut up: Many double-walled cities of that time had intricate, heavily fortified gate systems. Such strong cities as Jericho were not easily defeated, and the normal military strategy would have been to lay siege for several months or more, waiting for the people's food or water to run out.

because of the children of Israel: The kings of the entire land had heard how the Lord had dried up the Jordan River, and they were melted with fear—"there was no spirit in them any longer because of the children of Israel" (Joshua 5:1). Though the Lord had worked the great miracle of drying up the river primarily for the benefit of His people, He had also performed this wonder so that the world around them would see and believe that He alone was the God of all creation.

2. I have given Jericho into your hand: The Lord repeatedly gave the Israelites complete victory over the cities of Canaan. The phrase generally indicated that the Israelites were to completely defeat their enemies, often without leaving any survivors.

3. march around the city: This daily march openly demonstrated to the residents of Jericho, as well as her neighbors, that the Israelites were holding the city captive. Yet their obvious lack of military action would have been extremely puzzling to observers. It was a very public statement that the people of Israel were depending on God, rather than their own military might, to deliver the city.

you shall go all around the city once: The city of Jericho occupied approximately seven acres of land, so the march around it would not have taken very long.

4. trumpets of rams' horns: Rams' horns were used in combat as well as in religious exercises to gather the people together. The ark of the covenant went with the people in their march around the walls, indicating to the entire world that it was the Lord Himself who was leading Israel.

the seventh day you shall march around the city seven times: The number seven in Scripture often represents completion. For example, the Lord created the entire universe in six days, then rested on the seventh day (Genesis 2:1–3).

5. all the people shall shout: That the people were to shout is noteworthy. It indicated that a great triumph was about to be wrought. At the end of earth's history, "the Lord Himself will descend from heaven with a shout, with the voice of an archangel, and with the trumpet of God" (1 Thessalonians 4:16).

10. or make any noise with your voice: This was similar to the command to the people to stay back from the ark as they crossed the Jordan. It was a sign of meekness and reverence in the presence of the Lord, and it also provided the people a chance to meditate quietly upon the character of God as they marched around the walls. It also must have been extremely disconcerting to the people inside those walls to watch the silent procession.

THE WALLS COME TUMBLING DOWN: *The people of Israel follow the Lord's instructions exactly, and He works a powerful miracle on their behalf.*

17. DOOMED BY THE LORD TO DESTRUCTION: The Lord had literally devoted to ruin the entire city of Jericho. This concept is found frequently in the book of Joshua and elsewhere in the Old Testament, and it referred to consecrating something (such as pottery and other objects) to complete destruction as a sacrifice to the Lord. Cities such as Jericho had sunk themselves so deeply into wickedness that the Lord demanded their absolute obliteration—not only their material possessions, but every living thing, as well.

RAHAB THE HARLOT: Rahab entered the book of Joshua as a harlot, but she finished her life for the Lord, and was even in the lineage of Jesus. We will look at her in Study 6.

18. ABSTAIN FROM THE ACCURSED THINGS: The people of Jericho had become so wicked in the Lord's sight that even their possessions were corrupted, and God was determined that His people keep themselves pure from such taint. Joshua warned the people in strong terms: "by all means" they should keep themselves away from the "things" of Jericho.

LEST YOU BECOME ACCURSED WHEN YOU TAKE OF THE ACCURSED THINGS: To associate in any way with those whom God had placed under judgment—even to the point of taking away loot from their destruction—was to make oneself accursed along with those whom God had cursed. This stern warning was well warranted, as we will see when we look at the sin of Achan (Study 10).

20. THE WALL FELL DOWN FLAT: Archaeological studies have found that the city of Jericho probably existed during a time of several earthquakes, and it is possible that the Lord used such natural forces to bring down the city's walls, and perhaps also to dam up the Jordan River. But if such natural disasters were used, they were still not the cause of Jericho's miraculous devastation—it was the Lord Himself who brought down the walls, and whatever means He may have used to accomplish the miracle do not lessen His sovereignty.

22. AS YOU SWORE TO HER: Joshua took great care to ensure that he kept his word—even though he had not given his word directly. Two spies had promised Rahab that she and her family would be kept safe, provided that they remained in her house, and Joshua accepted their promise as binding. God's children are to be people of their word.

26. CURSED BE THE MAN: This terrible curse came to pass many centuries later when a man named Hiel attempted to rebuild the city's walls and gates, at the cost of his sons' lives (1 Kings 16:34).

ᴥ First Impressions ᴥ

1. If you had been with the Israelites, how would you have felt about marching around Jericho every day?

2. If you had been inside the city of Jericho, how would you have felt while watching the Israelites marching each day?

3. *Why did the people of Jericho lock themselves inside the city? Why did they not charge out and attack the Israelites?*

4. *Why did the Lord have the people carry the ark with them? Why did they blow rams' horns? Why were they not permitted to speak?*

↵ Some Key Principles ↵

Obey the Lord's commands, even if they don't address your immediate concerns.

Joshua and the Israelites were immediately concerned with the city of Jericho. It was a powerfully fortified city that lay directly in their path into Canaan, and they could not afford to leave it standing at their back as they entered the promised land. They needed to conquer that great city—but the Lord commanded them to spend a week marching around it, blowing horns. This must have seemed a strange command at the time.

Yet the Lord had His own plans for Jericho, and He wanted the people of Israel and the world around to see conclusively that He was the one who had knocked down its walls. His command to march around the wall was not frivolous, even though the people of Israel probably did not see the full meaning of it. Their job was to obey, not to comprehend the mind of God.

The Lord's commands frequently go directly against what the world teaches, and there can be times when God's people cannot see the full reason for obeying His Word. After all, the Bible was written thousands of years ago; it is easy at times to assume that its commands and precepts are not relevant today. But the Lord's Word stands for all time, and His commands are as relevant to Christians in the twenty-first century as they were when they were first penned. It may not be evident how obedience to God's Word will resolve a difficult situation in your life, but our job is to obey what the Bible teaches and trust the Lord to take care of our circumstances.

Let the Lord fight the battles.

The Israelites were commanded by God to enter the land of Canaan and to subdue it. This frequently involved warfare, and God's people needed to learn how to fight. But the battle was the Lord's, not theirs, whether their part involved taking up arms or merely marching around a city's walls and blowing ram's horns.

The Christian's warfare is mostly of a spiritual nature, as we are called to fight against spiritual forces rather than against other people. It is easy sometimes to lose sight of this fact, however, as our lives are frequently affected by the actions of people around us. The Lord wants His people to live responsibly, and we should take whatever actions we can within His will. But the battles we face are the Lord's, whether or not there is anything we can do on a human level. He wants us to place our faith in His sovereignty, remembering that the outcome of our lives is entirely in His hands.

Hear these words from Deuteronomy: "The LORD your God, who goes before you, He will fight for you, according to all He did for you in Egypt before your eyes, and in the wilderness where you saw how the LORD your God carried you, as a man carries his son, in all the way that you went until you came to this place" (1:30–31).

God's people are to keep themselves pure from the world's pollution.

The Lord had condemned the entire city of Jericho because of the wickedness of its people, and His condemnation extended even to the citizens' possessions and livestock. Everything had to be destroyed, because it was all tainted with corruption. God also commanded His people to refrain from keeping any plunder, lest they, too, be led into wickedness through the idols and other evil things they might find.

This principle is very important in the lives of modern Christians, because we are not a separate nation—we live in the world and must interact with it in some measure. Yet the Lord called His people to be *in* the world, not *of* it, not partaking in the sinful nature of the world's system. To stand guard against impurity requires our constant diligence, lest we gradually come to love the things of the world and lose sight of our calling to holiness.

"Do not love the world," wrote the apostle John, "or the things in the world. If anyone loves the world, the love of the Father is not in him. For all that is in the world—the lust of the flesh, the lust of the eyes, and the pride of life—is not of the Father but is of the world. And the world is passing away, and the lust of it; but he who does the will of God abides forever" (1 John 2:15–17).

⌁ DIGGING DEEPER ⌁

5. *Why did the Lord conquer Jericho the way He did? Why did He not have the Israelites attack outright?*

6. Why did the Lord command the Israelites to completely destroy the city, including the people's possessions? Why were the Israelites not to take any of the spoils?

7. In what ways does the world sometimes lead Christians into corruption today? Give specific examples.

8. What steps should Christians take to avoid being corrupted by the world?

9. What battles in your life have you been trying to fight for yourself? How can you leave those battles in the Lord's hands this week?

10. Are there areas in your life that have become corrupted by the world's values? What must you do to purify those areas?

3
THE SUN STANDS STILL

∽ HISTORICAL BACKGROUND ∽

By this time, the Lord had led Joshua and the Israelites to great victories over Jericho and Ai, and word had spread throughout Canaan that Israel's God was fighting on her behalf. The people of Canaan were filled with terror as they realized they could not possibly stand against the wrath of the almighty God.

Most of the cities of Canaan had responded to this threat by aggressively attacking Israel in hopes of defeating her armies before the Lord could intervene. One city, however, had adopted a different approach: the people of Gibeon had wisely determined to make peace, recognizing that they could not win if they remained enemies of Israel. But instead of asking for peace directly, they resorted to subterfuge, pretending that they lived very far away and posed no threat to God's people. The leaders of Israel were deceived by this ruse and signed a covenant in God's name that they would live at peace with Gibeon.

Meanwhile, the king of Jerusalem had formed an alliance with four other kings, and they were desperately trying to form a plan to defeat Israel. When they learned of Gibeon's peace covenant, they decided that their best course of action was to attack Israel's friends rather than Israel herself. But God honored Israel's covenant with Gibeon, and He would not allow the Canaanite kings to defeat that city any more than He would permit His own people to be destroyed.

So the Lord commanded Joshua to attack the five kings and their armies, ordering them to be of good courage. Israel's armies were probably outnumbered, and they arrived at the scene of battle already exhausted from an all-night uphill march—but the Lord Himself intended to fight the battle, so it didn't matter what the odds were against Israel. God showed Himself faithful and omnipotent that day, proving that there was nothing He could not or would not do for the sake of His people—even to the point of moving heaven and earth on Israel's behalf.

⌁ Reading Joshua 10:1–25 ⌁

Canaan Is Filled with Fear: *The people of Canaan have heard about what the Lord did to the city of Jericho, and they are filled with fear as the Israelites approach.*

1. Jerusalem: In the time of Joshua, this important city may have still been called Salem rather than Jerusalem. It was an important city in Abraham's day as well, when Melchizedek was its king. In Genesis 14, we read that Melchizedek came out and met Abraham (then called Abram) as he returned from rescuing his nephew Lot. In fact, this king (and by virtue of his position, his kingdom) blessed Abraham. The city's attitude toward Abraham's descendants, however, was vastly different. The Lord had promised that He would bless those who blessed Israel, and curse those who cursed Israel. The city of Salem had stood for hundreds of years, and had even prospered, but now its people were setting themselves against Israel, and its days were numbered.

Gibeon had made peace with Israel: The people of Gibeon recognized that the Lord was with the Israelites, and they knew that they could not stand before God's power. So they decided to make peace with Israel, using deception rather than straightforward surrender (Joshua 9).

2. they feared greatly: The people of Jerusalem were wise to fear the power of Israel, because Israel's might came directly from God, and He was tearing down all those cities that had devoted themselves to pagan gods. Still, Jerusalem's people deluded themselves with the belief that they could defeat the power of God simply by forming an alliance with their neighbors. Gibeon's inhabitants showed themselves to be wiser by humbling themselves and seeking peace.

3. Hebron . . . Jarmuth . . . Lachish . . . Eglon: See the map in the Introduction.

Attack Against Gibeon: *The Canaanite kings are afraid to attack Israel outright, so they do the next best thing: they attack Israel's allies.*

4. that we may attack Gibeon: Those who make peace with God, or even just with God's people, open themselves to the attack of God's enemies. The Canaanite kings may have recognized that they could not defeat Israel in direct combat, but they evidently thought they could discourage other cities from making peace. This thinking continues to the present day, as many nations in the Middle East conspire to destroy Israel, considering any nation who helps Israel as their enemy. But God had promised to bless those who bless Israel, and He did not permit these kings to destroy Gibeon.

6. Do not forsake your servants: The people of Israel had actually made a mistake when they formed a covenant with the inhabitants of Gibeon, as they were deceived into thinking that the Gibeonites lived far away. Worse, they did not seek the Lord's counsel on the matter (Joshua 9:14) and ended up in an alliance that should not have been made. Nevertheless, the Lord honored that covenant and protected the people of Gibeon—despite their treacherous deception. The Gibeonites held a long-standing alliance with Israel, even helping to rebuild Jerusalem in the time of Nehemiah (Nehemiah 3:7).

Do Not Be Afraid: *The Lord tells Joshua that He will fight Israel's battles and will give them great victory. Their part is only to trust and obey.*

8. Do not fear them: This commandment appears frequently in the book of Joshua. It is significant that it is a command, rather than a mere word of encouragement, like "Cheer up." The Lord *commands* His people to resist fear, to choose deliberately to stand strong in courage. Ultimately, our courage is drawn from the character of God: we choose to place our faith in Him, because we know that He is faithful. Giving in to fear, therefore, is a lack of faith in His character. Fear is what motivated the people of Jerusalem and other Canaanite cities—they had no faith in the God of Israel and therefore fell prey to their own terror.

9. having marched all night from Gilgal: Gilgal was approximately twenty miles from Gibeon, and the march was mostly uphill.

10. the Lord routed them: The word translated "routed" implies that the enemy was thrown into great confusion and panic. Here we see the result of the armies' fear, in contrast to the great courage of the Israelites. When we place our trust in God and stand firm against fear, the Lord will prove Himself faithful. This is the key to being victorious in the Christian life. The Israelites' victory was all the more dramatic after an all-night march uphill, carrying their weapons and gear. They would have been fatigued prior to the fight, but the battle was fought on their behalf by the Lord Himself.

Two Great Miracles: *God sends great hailstones on the enemy, and then He causes the sun to stand still in the sky.*

11. more . . . died from the hailstones: This is direct evidence that the battle was being fought by the Lord, not by Israel's military might. Joshua and his army needed to be present during the battle, as the Lord had commanded them to fight, but the ultimate victory was not won through their military prowess.

13. THE SUN STOOD STILL: Many scholars have attempted to explain away what occurred on this day, suggesting that there was an eclipse of the sun, or that the author was only speaking poetically rather than literally. Yet there is no question that the author (probably Joshua himself) was speaking literally, recounting a literal historical event. The only plausible explanation, therefore, is that the Lord miraculously caused the earth to pause in its rotation and the moon to briefly halt in its orbit. This is one of the most dramatic miracles in the Old Testament—and yet it pales in comparison with the miracles of the New Testament, where God Himself became a man, born of a virgin; where God the Son resurrected those who were dead; where God the Father resurrected His Son from the dead; and where the resurrected Son offered salvation to those who had no hope and who were already dead in their sins. Those who have placed their faith in the salvation plan of Christ should have no trouble placing their faith in a miracle that is simple by comparison, such as the sun standing still—or any other marvel He performs.

25. BE STRONG AND OF GOOD COURAGE: Here again we find the command to resist fear, choosing rather to be strong and of good courage. We tend to think of fear as an emotion, a reflexive response over which we have no control—but that is not what the Scriptures teach. We are commanded—not merely encouraged—to be strong, to fill our hearts and minds with courage, even when we are faced with circumstances that urge us to be afraid. Courage is a deliberate choice, not an instinctive response or some innate ability that some people have and others don't. All of God's people are charged to choose strength and courage instead of fear and weakness. This is accomplished by deliberately electing to place our faith in God's sovereignty and faithfulness. He defeated the enemies of Israel in the past, and He will defeat the enemies of His people in the future.

∽ First Impressions ∾

1. *Why did the Canaanite kings attack Gibeon rather than Israel? What principle does this illustrate concerning the world's attitude toward God's people?*

2. *Why did God use hailstones to defeat the Canaanite armies? Why not just allow Joshua's army to win the battle outright?*

3. *Why did Joshua command the sun to stand still? What did this reveal about his faith?*

4. *Why did God honor Joshua's bold command? What does this reveal about His character?*

Some Key Principles

God can literally move heaven and earth to accomplish His purposes.

Or, to speak more specifically to the events discussed in this chapter, the Lord can cause the earth and heavens (the atmosphere) to *not* move. In order for the sun to "stand still," the earth itself would have needed to stop revolving on its axis—and evidently this is exactly what the Lord did for the Israelites on that momentous day. He literally caused the earth to stop for a period of hours simply so that His people might have victory in battle.

The Lord went beyond even this "earthshaking" miracle when He moved heaven itself—the abode of God—to send His Son to earth as a man. He temporarily set aside the laws of biology, causing a virgin to become pregnant with the Son of God. More than this, He permitted His Holy One to take on the sin of mankind; He caused the One who is Life to taste death; He subjected the Creator to the whims of those He had created. And He did all of this so that we might be reconciled with Himself.

If God would do all of this for the sake of sinful people, He will certainly prove faithful in meeting your present needs. Some problems may be too great for your power to resolve, but there is no problem too great for God.

Do not be afraid, but be strong and of good courage.

This commandment appears frequently in the book of Joshua—usually at times when there seemed to be genuine cause for fear. The army of Israel had marched all night long, uphill, carrying all their battle gear. They had arrived to face not one but five enemy armies, and they were already tired before the battle even began. Yet the Lord commanded His people to not give in to fear.

Fear is the enemy of God's people. It moves us away from faith, and toward disobedience. The people of Israel, for example, arrived at the Jordan River, ready to take possession of the promised land, but their spies brought back a discouraging report: there were giants in the land, and fortified cities! The Israelites then yielded to fear and disobeyed the Lord, dooming that entire generation to die in the wilderness without entering the promised land (Numbers 13–14).

We are commanded to resist fear, which demonstrates that fear is something we can master. This is done by shifting our focus away from the situation that threatens us and focusing on the Lord who redeems us. He is absolutely sovereign over all our affairs, and He is completely faithful to save His people. If He was willing to make the sun stand still for Israel's army, He will be willing to intervene in your life as well.

God blesses those who bless Israel.

All the people of Canaan were filled with terror at the approach of Israel, because they all knew what the Lord had done on their behalf at Jericho. Most of those cities responded with violence, attempting to make war against God's people—with one notable exception: the people of Gibeon sought to make peace. Their methods were perverse—they used trickery to deceive Joshua into making a covenant of peace, yet the Lord honored that covenant and allowed the Gibeonites to remain in Canaan.

This principle goes far back in history to the time of Abraham. God promised Abraham (then called Abram), "I will bless those who bless you, and I will curse him who curses you; and in you all the families of the earth shall be blessed" (Genesis 12:3). The Lord proved Himself faithful to that promise again and again throughout the Old Testament, and the promise is still in effect today.

Much of the modern world has arrayed itself against the nation of Israel. There is constant turmoil in the Middle East, as many of the Arab nations seethe with anger and plot to bring about the destruction of the Jews. But in the long run, God will prove absolutely loyal to His promise of old, and He will bring destruction upon those nations that set themselves against Israel. He will also one day bring the Jewish nation to a saving knowledge of the Messiah, Jesus Christ (Romans 11:26).

↳ DIGGING DEEPER ↲

5. *Why did the people of Gibeon use deception to make peace with Israel? Why did God honor Israel's covenant with them anyway?*

6. *Why does God command His people to be strong and of good courage? In what way is strength a matter of choice? In what way is courage a matter of choice?*

7. *Do you believe that God actually caused the earth to stop rotating on its axis for a period of time? Why or why not? What does your response reveal about your faith?*

8. Why does God bless those who bless Israel? How does this promise apply today in the ongoing Middle East conflicts?

ᴄ Taking It Personally ᴄ

9. When you are faced with a crisis, what is your response? How courageous are you? Where do you place your hope for a solution?

10. Do you believe that God, who moved heaven and earth for Israel, stands on your behalf? How can you strengthen your faith in His character?

4
RAISING UP JUDGES

⌁ HISTORICAL BACKGROUND ⌁

The people of Israel entered the promised land with great joy and tremendous victory. They had witnessed the power of their God through incredible miracles, such as the parting of the Jordan River and the sun standing still, as well as through miraculous victories over their enemies. There could be no doubt that the Lord was sovereign and that He was fighting on their behalf.

But in all of those great miracles and victories, the Lord had commanded the people to be involved. They had not sat on the sidelines, merely watching the walls of Jericho collapse; they had marched around the city and blown trumpets for seven days. The Lord made the sun stand still and sent huge hailstones to defeat Israel's enemies, but He had also insisted that Israel fight in the battle. God was fighting Israel's battles on her behalf, but the people still needed to walk in obedience to His commands.

One of those commands had been to drive out all the people of Canaan and to tear down their pagan altars. The people got off to a good start under the leadership of Joshua, moving from battle to battle and victory to victory. But as time went along, the various tribes of Israel gradually began to fail. Rather than driving out the Canaanites, they used them as slaves and permitted them to remain in the land.

After Joshua died, the Israelites began a long period of falling into paganism, followed by repentance, followed by a relapse into paganism. During this time, the Lord raised up a succession of individuals known as *judges*, men and one woman who led the nation to victory over her enemies and back toward obedience to God. Yet the cycle of sin and repentance continued.

THE LORD DISCIPLINES HIS PEOPLE: *Israel had been commanded to drive out the Canaanites and to destroy their pagan worship sites, but they had failed to do so.*

1. THE ANGEL OF THE LORD: Once again, the Lord Himself appeared to the people of Israel—but this time His message was not good news.

BOCHIM: This location is not certain, but it may have been near Bethel.

2. YOU SHALL MAKE NO COVENANT WITH THE INHABITANTS OF THIS LAND: The Lord had also told the people, "I will set your bounds from the Red Sea to the sea, Philistia, and from the desert to the River. For I will deliver the inhabitants of the land into your hand, and you shall drive them out before you. You shall make no covenant with them, nor with their gods (Exodus 23:31–32). The people of Israel did not obey the Lord's command in this regard. They had scarcely arrived in the promised land when they made a covenant with the people of Gibeon. This is exactly what God had forbidden. "They shall not dwell in your land," He had said, "lest they make you sin against Me. For if you serve their gods, it will surely be a snare to you" (v. 33). And it was.

YOU SHALL TEAR DOWN THEIR ALTARS: The Lord had made a similar command prior to the battle against Jericho, when He told the people, "By all means abstain from the accursed things, lest you become accursed when you take of the accursed things, and make the camp of Israel a curse, and trouble it" (Joshua 6:18). It was not enough merely to defeat the Lord's enemies in Canaan; the Israelites were also to completely destroy anything that pertained to the Canaanites' pagan practices.

YOU HAVE NOT OBEYED MY VOICE: Judges 1 gives further detail on this. Most of the tribes of Israel had taken possession of areas of Canaan, but they had failed to drive out the former inhabitants. Many of the Canaanite nations were put under tribute to the tribes of Israel, effectively serving them as slaves. The Israelites may have thought that enslaving the people of Canaan was "close enough" to the Lord's command; it may even have seemed both merciful and prudent to gain labor from them rather than killing them or driving them out. But the Lord had specifically and repeatedly told the people to not make any form of treaty with the Canaanites—not even one involving slavery—and they had disobeyed Him.

3. I WILL NOT DRIVE THEM OUT BEFORE YOU: The people of Israel may have lost sight of the fact that their great victories in battle were the Lord's doing, not their own. It was the Lord who had destroyed Jericho and defeated Ai, God Himself who had made the sun stand still and the Jordan River part. Yet in each of these great victories, He had also commanded the people to participate in some small way. Their marching around the walls of Jericho and blowing trumpets had not caused the walls to collapse; but at the same time, had they not obeyed the Lord's commands in that battle, He would not have brought down the walls. Now they had failed to do their part, driving out the Canaanites, so the Lord would withdraw His arm from their battles as well.

THEIR GODS SHALL BE A SNARE TO YOU: This is the reason the Lord had commanded Israel to drive out the Canaanites and to destroy their altars. God did not take pleasure in destroying the nations of Canaan, and He did not command His people to do so out of some vindictive, spiteful spirit. The people of Canaan had given themselves fully to paganism and were devoted to all manner of false gods and wicked worship practices, and it was this that the Lord wanted to destroy. God is jealous of His people's purity, and He knew that the Canaanites' religion would corrupt the Israelites if it were allowed to remain. Thus, He commanded that the pagans be driven out and their idolatrous altars be completely destroyed. When the Israelites failed to obey, they opened the door to all manner of corruption.

4. THE PEOPLE LIFTED UP THEIR VOICES AND WEPT: Recognizing that the Lord's hand of discipline was upon them, due to their many years of disobedience and indifference, the people wept.

5. BOCHIM: Meaning "weepers."

THE NEXT GENERATION: *The people of Israel had failed to teach their children about the Lord's character and all that He had done for them. The consequences came quickly.*

10. DID NOT KNOW THE LORD: In Study 1, we looked at the stone monument that the Lord commanded His people to build after crossing the Jordan, "that this may be a sign among you when your children ask in time to come, saying, 'What do these stones mean to you?'" (Joshua 4:6). Here we see the reason for that monument, as the subsequent generations in Israel had apparently failed to teach their children about all the Lord had done. It didn't take long before a generation arose who had no knowledge of the Lord's character or the mighty miracles He had performed on behalf of His people. The same trend is happening in our world today.

11. DID EVIL IN THE SIGHT OF THE LORD: This is the natural result of failing to train one's children in the ways of the Lord. If we don't actively teach righteousness to the next generation, they will naturally fall into evil—especially in the pagan ways of the world around them. This generation of Israelites began to worship Baal, a pagan God served by the Canaanites who had not been driven out of the land.

13. BAAL AND THE ASHTORETHS: Baal was one of the chief false deities worshipped in Canaan. He was pictured as standing astride a bull and was thought to provide spring rains and abundant crops. The Ashtoreths were various false goddesses, including Ashtoreth (consort of Baal) and Asherah (wife of Baal's father), who were believed to bring fertility and military strength. The pagan worship rites of all of these counterfeit gods included temple prostitution and even child sacrifice.

14. DELIVERED THEM INTO THE HANDS OF PLUNDERERS: When Israel was following the Lord in obedience, He delivered her enemies into her hands; but when Israel abandoned the Lord, He delivered her to her enemies. This was done not to destroy Israel but to bring her back to the Lord and to purify her of pagan immorality.

THE LORD RAISES UP JUDGES: *Even in the midst of God's discipline, His grace and mercy abound. He raises up judges in Israel to lead His people back to obedience.*

16. THE LORD RAISED UP JUDGES: The Lord did send calamity upon Israel when she abandoned Him, but here we see that His discipline was meant for the good of His people. He showed His mercy, even in the midst of His discipline, by providing judges who would lead His people back to obedience. These judges were gifted leaders, raised up by the Lord at various times and in a variety of locations in Israel's history. Many of them led Israel's fighting forces to military victory, and some also provided legal judgment among the Israelites. There were six "minor" judges (meaning that the Bible gives little detail about them) and six "major" judges (Othniel, Ehud, Deborah, Gideon, Jephthah, and Samson). We will look at several of these people in the Characters studies.

17. THEY WOULD NOT LISTEN TO THEIR JUDGES: The people of Israel had a long history of not listening to their God-appointed leaders. They had repeatedly refused to listen to Moses and more than once rose up in rebellion against his leadership. When God's people reject the leadership God has appointed, we are effectively rejecting the lordship of God Himself.

THEY PLAYED THE HARLOT WITH OTHER GODS: The Lord views idolatry of any kind as a form of spiritual adultery. His people belong to Him alone, and we become like an unfaithful wife when we permit anything to come between us and Him.

18. THE LORD WAS MOVED TO PITY BY THEIR GROANING: The Lord sent a series of calamities and hardships to Israel during this time period (roughly 450 years), but His motivation was always the same: to bring His people back to Himself. God does not take pleasure in disciplining His children, and He is always moved to pity when He hears our heartfelt groans.

19. WHEN THE JUDGE WAS DEAD: This was a continual cycle in Israel during these years. The people would abandon the Lord and run after pagan gods; the Lord would deliver Israel into the hands of her enemies; the people would cry out in despair under the Lord's discipline; the Lord would have mercy and raise up a judge to deliver Israel; the people would obey the Lord for a time; the judge would die . . . and the cycle would begin again. The great wonder of this sequence is that the Lord continued to show grace and patience with such obstinate sinners. Sadly, we are no different from the Israelites, and we must guard against imitating their cycle of sin and repentance.

⌁ First Impressions ⌁

1. *Why did God command Israel to not make any covenants with the people of Canaan? What resulted from their failure to obey?*

2. *Why had the people not driven out the Canaanites, as God commanded? What motivated their disobedience?*

3. If you had been present when the angel of the Lord pronounced God's discipline, how would you have reacted? How would it have influenced your life in the future?

4. Why were the people commanded to tear down the Canaanites' altars? What resulted from that disobedience?

⤳ Some Key Principles ⤳

The world's values can become a snare to God's people.

The Lord had commanded the Israelites to completely drive out the people of Canaan because the Canaanites had devoted themselves to pagan practices. Furthermore, He had insisted that Israel also destroy the worship sites where the Canaanites had conducted their pagan rites, because He knew that His people could be seduced into idolatry by long-term contact with those who worshipped idols.

The same principle holds true today. The modern world has increasingly embraced all forms of paganism, and its value system is opposed to the Word of God. A Christian can easily be lured away from purity and obedience by the world's emphasis on the pursuit of pleasure, self-worship, sexual immorality, and materialism. The process of embracing those values can also be subtle and gradual, a process of small steps that seem innocuous at the time.

The way to stand guard against this danger is to be constantly renewing our minds with the truth. It is vital to spend time daily reading God's Word and talking with Him in prayer. Joining with other Christians, on a regular basis, for worship and teaching (through involvement with a local church) is also essential. The Holy Spirit is our guard against the pagan influences of the world, but we are called to do our part in obeying the Bible's teachings.

Our present generation is growing up without spiritual guidance.

God commanded His people to be faithful in teaching their children about His character and His involvement with Israel. He had them build a monument after crossing the Jordan for the specific purpose of teaching the next generation about what He had done to bring them into the promised land. But the Israelites gradually forgot to follow this principle, and eventually a generation grew up who didn't know the Lord at all.

The result of this failure was that an entire generation in Israel wandered away from obedience to God and embraced the pagan practices of the world around them. In a way, that was only to be expected, because that generation had not been adequately taught about who God is or what He expected of His people. Their parents had not properly instructed them about God, and thus they were seduced by the pagan religions of Canaan.

Western civilization today is seeing a generation coming to adulthood who know nothing about God's character or what He expects of men and women. These young adults have no root in God's Word, no direction on what the Creator expects of His people, so they naturally follow the pagan teachings of the world around them. It is vital that Christians today be bold in teaching the next generation the truth of the Bible.

Do not fall into a cycle of sin and repentance.

The people of Israel had disobeyed the Lord's commands, and this led them into idolatry and immorality. The Lord responded by sending hardship upon the people as a form of discipline, urging them to return to obedience and purity. The oppression of enemies and other calamities forced Israel to repent and return to the Lord, and He graciously sent judges to lead them back to obedience. But after a time, the people lost interest in the things of God and soon began the cycle all over again.

This cycle was not pleasing to God. He wants His people to obey Him willingly, to worship Him voluntarily with their whole hearts.

God will send discipline into the lives of His children to make us purer and more like Christ, but His deep desire is that we obey Him out of love and gratitude, rather than by the compulsion of hardship. It is a mark of spiritual maturity to obey God's Word simply because we know that it pleases and glorifies the Father.

⌁ Digging Deeper ⌁

5. How might the Israelites have justified their failure to drive out the people of Canaan? In what ways do Christians today sometimes justify disobedience and worldliness?

6. Why did the Lord respond to Israel's disobedience by not driving out the Canaanites? What might have resulted if He had driven them out?

7. *Why did a generation grow up without knowing God? What evidence do you see of that trend in the world today? What can be done to correct that?*

8. *What sorts of "snares" endanger a Christian today? How can we guard against them?*

9. What motivates you to obey God's Word? Are you in a cycle of sin and repentance, or do you obey willingly?

10. Are you ensnared with the world's values? What areas in your life might the Lord want you to purify in the coming week?

~ 5 ~
RUTH AND BOAZ

↬ HISTORICAL BACKGROUND ↫

The people of Israel had been living in the promised land for several generations, during the time known as the period of the judges. The land of Judah was experiencing a famine. No further details are known about this famine, yet we do know that it was severe enough for a man named Elimelech to move his family to the land of Moab, east of the Dead Sea.

The Moabites were descendants of Lot from an incestuous union with his oldest daughter (Genesis 19). Their relations with Israel had not been good, and the Lord had forbidden the Moabites from entering the congregation. Yet Elimelech moved his wife and two sons to a land that was hostile to God's people—and he married his sons to Moabite women.

Many years later, after Elimelech's death, his widow, Naomi, returned to Judah, arriving during the barley harvest. The harvest was a time of hard physical labor, involving cutting the grain by hand, binding it into sheaves, and threshing out the edible grain from the chaff. During this process, the poor were permitted to walk through harvested fields, picking up any bits of grain that had been left behind by the harvesters. The law of Moses required farmers to leave behind certain portions of grain for the sake of the poor who would come to glean. The law, however, did not require farmers to feed the gleaners or to pay them any special attention—to do that would be to go above and beyond the call of duty.

In this background we meet Ruth and Boaz, and we are privileged to read one of the greatest romantic stories in the Bible. Ruth and Boaz were destined to be together—literally a match made in heaven. Through their descendants, God would bring about the human birth of His Son, Jesus Christ.

↢ Reading Ruth 1:1–22 ↣

Two Weddings and Three Funerals: *A family moves to Moab to escape famine, and the sons marry Moabite women. The men die, leaving three widows behind.*

1. Moab: The Moabites were descended from Lot, who had committed incest with his daughters after the destruction of Sodom and Gomorrah. Their land was east of the Dead Sea. (See the map in the Introduction.) The passage does not tell us whether Elimelech was justified in moving to Moab, since he was effectively leaving the promised land to live with the Canaanites.

4. they took wives of the women of Moab: The Lord had expressly forbidden the Israelites from marrying Canaanites (Deuteronomy 7:1–3), and the Moabites in particular were excluded from the congregation of Israel (Deuteronomy 23:3–6). These marriages were questionable at best. Nevertheless, the Lord would bring great good out of one marriage: Ruth was destined to be in the family line of Jesus.

5. the woman survived her two sons and her husband: This tragedy would have been grievous enough for anyone to endure, but Naomi's sorrow was compounded by the fact that she had no sons to carry on the family name. We will come back to this theme in Study 11 when we consider the Kinsman Redeemer.

6. the Lord had visited His people: The sovereignty of God is seen throughout this book, as the Lord worked to bring about a good end to these tragic events.

Parting Company: *Naomi urges her daughters-in-law to return to their own families and find husbands for themselves.*

8. return each to her mother's house: Orpah and Ruth were Moabites and therefore had no place in the congregation of Israel. It was only natural that they should return to their families and remain in the land of Moab. Naomi at this point looked forward only to returning to Judah as a lonely widow, bereft of any offspring. Her future was very bleak.

11. Turn back, my daughters: Naomi was being selfless in urging her daughters-in-law to go home to Moab. It would have been a comfort for her to have their company on the return trip to Judah, but she was more concerned for their future and welfare. She wanted them to find husbands and have families to carry on their family heritage.

13. the hand of the Lord has gone out against me: We can certainly understand the terrible grief Naomi must have been suffering at this time. Nevertheless, her perspective was inaccurate. The Lord had not set His hand against her, as later events would make clear. Though unpleasant in the short-term, suffering and trials are used by God to make His people more like Himself. Peter confirmed this when he wrote, "In this you greatly rejoice, though now for a little while, if need be, you have been grieved by various trials, that the genuineness of your faith, being much more precious than gold that perishes, though it is tested by fire, may be found to praise, honor, and glory at the revelation of Jesus Christ" (1 Peter 1:6–7).

15. BACK TO HER PEOPLE AND TO HER GODS: Orpah's decision to return to Moab probably seemed prudent at the time, as it was more likely that she would find a husband and family there. But the bigger issue is that her return to Moab was also a return to Moab's gods, and was thus a rejection of the God of Israel. (The chief deity of Moab was Chemosh, whose worship included child sacrifice.)

> **RUTH REMAINS:** *Orpah has gone back to her family in Moab, but Ruth refuses to leave the side of her mother-in-law. She is willing to abandon everything in her faithfulness.*

16. WHEREVER YOU GO, I WILL GO: Ruth's commitment to follow Naomi is often used in modern wedding vows. Yet it is more than beautiful poetry. Her words expressed a complete commitment to remain with Naomi, regardless of her circumstances.

YOUR GOD, MY GOD: Ruth recognized that her decision to move to Judah included a resolve to forsake the gods of Moab and to instead embrace the God of Israel, the Lord of creation. This conversion had consequences for the entire human race, as her family line would lead ultimately to the person of Jesus.

20. CALL ME MARA: Naomi means "pleasant," while Mara means "bitter." Upon her return to Judah, Naomi expressed the bitterness in her soul—and in the process, she wrongly concluded that God was "testif[ying]" against her (v. 21). But God had not abandoned Naomi, no matter how overwhelming she found her trials to be. Though she had experienced much sorrow, she would soon experience great blessing according to God's perfect plan.

ᴧ READING RUTH 2:1–12 ᴧ

> **BACK IN JUDAH:** *Naomi and Ruth arrive in Judah, and Ruth immediately sets to work gathering food for them both. Then God reveals His loving, sovereign hand.*

2. RUTH THE MOABITESS: The author used this phrase repeatedly to remind the reader that Ruth was actually an outsider—one who had no right to be part of the congregation of Israel *at all*. It is a beautiful picture of God's grace, as He reaches out to those who are outside of salvation, even to those who deserve His grace the least, and brings us into His kingdom.

GLEAN HEADS OF GRAIN: The Mosaic law stipulated that God's people should deliberately leave behind certain portions of any harvest (Leviticus 19:9–10). This permitted the needy to come through a harvested field and pick up leftover grain or grapes, a process called *gleaning*.

3. SHE HAPPENED TO COME: Here again we see the sovereignty of God at work to bless His people. From a human perspective, Ruth just coincidentally selected the field of Boaz, who just coincidentally was Naomi's relative—and just coincidentally was very rich. But there was no coincidence involved at all. The Lord was leading Ruth to Boaz, and His plan of blessing extended far beyond Ruth's immediate family.

4. BOAZ CAME FROM BETHLEHEM: Here is another detail that appears, from a human perspective, to be mere coincidence. Boaz evidently lived in Bethlehem, and he just happened to choose that particular day to travel to his field to check on the harvest. But once again, it was the Lord's sovereign hand that deliberately orchestrated this historic meeting.

TWO GODLY CHARACTERS: *Boaz and Ruth meet, and each immediately recognizes godly character in the other. This couple's descendants will eventually lead to Jesus.*

7. SHE CAME AND HAS CONTINUED FROM MORNING UNTIL NOW: Ruth was a diligent worker, laboring tirelessly to provide for her mother-in-law.

8. MY DAUGHTER: Boaz was approximately the same age as Naomi, and was therefore old enough to be Ruth's father.

STAY CLOSE BY MY YOUNG WOMEN: Boaz went above and beyond what was required of him by the Mosaic law. He was only required to permit Ruth to glean what was left behind when the harvest was complete, generally after his workers had left the field. But he urged her to stay close to his employees and glean while they harvested, and pressed her to not move to anyone else's field. Later, he would instruct his young men to deliberately drop extra grain for her to pick up (v. 15–16). In this, Boaz demonstrated the spirit of God's law, being kind to strangers and caring for widows. "Pure and undefiled religion before God and the Father is this: to visit orphans and widows in their trouble, and to keep oneself unspotted from the world" (James 1:27).

10. WHY HAVE I FOUND FAVOR IN YOUR EYES?: Ruth remained humble, always remembering that she was in Judah only by special accommodation. She did not have the attitude that the world owed her something, despite the fact that she might have made a legitimate claim on Boaz's generosity because she had married into his family.

11. ALL THAT YOU HAVE DONE FOR YOUR MOTHER-IN-LAW: Ruth's generous character and diligence had earned her a reputation among the Israelites.

12. UNDER WHOSE WINGS YOU HAVE COME FOR REFUGE: Boaz stood in sharp contrast to Naomi, as he recognized the true nature of God's character. Naomi pictured God as a harsh judge, carefully meting out punishment upon her to the last bit of suffering. Boaz, on the other hand, recognized that God protects and cares for His children just as a mother hen covers her young with her wings—even to the point of sacrificing her own life on their behalf. This picture was perfectly fulfilled when God's Son gave His own life on the cross for our sake.

⮥ First Impressions ⮤

1. *If you had been in Naomi's position, how would you have responded when your husband and sons died in a foreign land?*

2. *If you had been in Orpah and Ruth's position, what would you have done when Naomi urged you to return to Moab?*

3.   *What character traits do you see in Ruth? In Boaz? In Naomi?*

4.   *Why did Boaz treat Ruth with so much kindness?*

ᚱ Some Key Principles ᚱ

God works all things together for good in the lives of His children.

Naomi endured much grief and suffering, fleeing her native land because of famine, moving to a strange land whose people worshipped false gods, and watching as her husband and two sons all died there. From a human perspective, one can easily understand how she would be overcome with sorrow, feeling that the Lord had dealt harshly with her.

Yet the Lord had tremendous blessing in store for her, which outweighed her loss. Her daughter-in-law turned away from the pagan gods of Moab and embraced the true God of Israel. Ruth was providentially brought together with Boaz, a wealthy and influential man in Israel. Boaz married her, providing Naomi with grandchildren and blessings that extended far into the future.

God's people are not exempt from sorrow and hardship, and all suffering seems grievous at the time. But we must remember that all things are under the sovereign control of God, and nothing can touch us that God Himself has not approved. He sends discipline and heartache into our lives to purify us and to make us more like Christ, but in the long run the blessings far outweigh the hardships. "And we know that all things work together for good to those who love God, to those who are the called according to His purpose" (Romans 8:28).

The Lord makes His salvation available to all people everywhere.

The Moabites were descended from Lot's incestuous relations with his daughters. Balak, a prince of Moab, had even attempted to put a curse on Israel by hiring Balaam (Numbers 22–25). For these reasons and more, God had forbidden the Moabites from entering the congregation of Israel. In many ways, the people of Moab were outcasts in the eyes of God's people.

But Ruth chose to forsake the gods of Moab and embrace the God of Israel, and in that moment she ceased to be an outcast and became a beloved child of God. She was welcomed into the land of Israel, and she discovered to her joy that the Lord had a breathtaking plan for her life and her descendants—and He had all the details worked out in advance.

Ruth went from being an outsider who had no hope of entering God's presence, to being included in the human line of Jesus. In the same way, any sinner who embraces God's salvation through Christ is instantly transformed from despair into joy, from outcast to inheritance, from death into life. This incomparable grace is available to all, no matter what your background, no matter what your sins, no matter what your past. There are no exceptions to this rule: God welcomes all who come to Him in sincere repentance.

God rewards our faithfulness.

Orpah and Ruth were faced with a difficult decision: should they follow Naomi to Judah or return to their families in Moab? Orpah followed what seemed the prudent course, returning to Moab in hopes of finding another husband and raising a family. Ruth, however, chose the more difficult path by opting to remain faithful to her mother-in-law. She was not obligated to do so, since her husband had died, yet she took seriously her marital commitment to remain part of her husband's family.

Both Ruth and Boaz demonstrated faithfulness. Ruth was diligent to gather cast-off grain, a task that was very lowly in that culture. Boaz fulfilled his duties to the law by permitting Ruth to glean in his field—then went far beyond what was required in looking after her and Naomi. Both Ruth and Boaz proved faithful in their obedience to God's Word and their loyalty to family.

This is the attitude God desires in all of His children, serving others out of a heart of humility and sincerity. He calls His people to give with a cheerful heart, to serve one another with a selfless spirit, and to show love without hypocrisy. He Himself set the example by washing His disciples' feet. "You shall love the Lord your God with all your heart, with all your soul, and with all your mind,'" He taught. "This is the first and great commandment. And the second is like it: 'You shall love your neighbor as yourself.' On these two commandments hang all the Law and the Prophets" (Matthew 22:37–40).

⌁ Digging Deeper ⌁

5. *Skim back through Ruth 1–2 and look for behind-the-scenes evidence of God's sovereign hand. How did He work out all the details for Naomi and Ruth?*

6. *What losses did Naomi suffer? What blessings did she gain?*

7. *What sort of treatment should Ruth have expected when she moved to Judah? What did she experience? Why?*

8. *Nothing further is known of Orpah. What does this suggest about her decision to stay in Moab? Why was this a poor decision?*

9. When have you seen God's hand of sovereignty working to bring blessings out of suffering? What areas of hardship are you experiencing now? What spiritual blessings might God be producing for the future?

10. Is your life characterized by faithfulness to God? In what areas might the Lord want you to be more faithful?

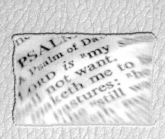

Section 2:

Characters

In This Section:

~ 6 ~
RAHAB

⌁ HISTORICAL BACKGROUND ⌁

We now return to the time prior to the fall of Jericho, before Israel had crossed the Jordan River. The Israelites were encamped at the acacia grove on the east side of the Jordan, and they were preparing to follow God in His miraculous parting of the waters. But Joshua was a strong military leader, and he wanted information about Jericho prior to facing the city in battle. To gain that information, he sent two spies into the city to learn more about its inhabitants and their defenses.

We are not told what those spies learned, because in the long run it didn't matter. God's plans for Jericho's destruction did not require any military prowess or human strategies. He would use supernatural means to destroy His enemies. But He would also bring salvation to one particular person who lived in that city, and He used the spies to reach her.

Jericho was surrounded by two walls, one behind the other. Between those walls were houses that were actually built into one or both walls, and those houses frequently had windows that opened through the city's defensive walls. Such houses were very simple and small, inhabited by the city's poor—and worse. Their location near the city gates, for example, would be a perfect place to carry on the business of prostitution. The constant traffic of people entering and leaving the city would be good for business, especially since it would be easy to enter and exit such a house unnoticed. This element of anonymity was also useful for the spies—it was unlikely that they would be noticed entering such a house of prostitution.

In Studies 1 and 2, we saw God working some very powerful and dramatic miracles, as He parted the Jordan River and made Jericho's formidable walls collapse. In this study, however, we will witness a miracle of greater power and drama: the Lord will redeem the life of a lowly Canaanite prostitute. In fact, He will go even beyond this miracle: He will transform that woman of sin into a woman of God, and her descendants will include Jesus Himself.

SPIES IN JERICHO: *Joshua sends two spies inside the city of Jericho to gather information. They hide themselves in the house of a prostitute.*

1. ACACIA GROVE: This passage occurred prior to the miraculous crossing of the Jordan River. This grove was on the east side of the river, and was used as a base camp.

CAME TO THE HOUSE OF A HARLOT: The two spies did not visit Rahab's house for any illicit purpose, but rather because it offered a good hiding place. They were spies of a hostile army, and as such went at risk of losing their lives if caught. They probably thought that strange men entering a prostitute's house would not be noticed. But it was actually the Lord who led them there, because He intended to rescue Rahab and redeem her to Himself.

4. HID THEM: At this point, Rahab made a risky decision from which there was no turning back. She would have been immediately put to death if the men had been discovered in her house. She had already made up her mind to join Israel and make their God her God, just as we saw Ruth do in the previous study.

5. THE MEN WENT OUT: Rahab lied in order to protect the Jews, probably considering it justified during a time of war. In the Lord's eyes, the ends do not justify the means—lying is a sin, and He never condones it. Nevertheless, God focused on Rahab's faith and her courageous decision to help His people.

6. HIDDEN THEM WITH THE STALKS OF FLAX: Houses in those days had flat roofs that were used for many purposes, including places to dry grains. Flax was used to make linen cloth.

TURNING TO GOD: *Rahab saves the spies because she recognizes that Israel serves the only true God, Creator of heaven and earth.*

9. I KNOW THAT THE LORD HAS GIVEN YOU THE LAND: Rahab revealed her motivation in what she said to the spies. Notice that she mentioned the Lord's name repeatedly. She recognized that Israel's great victories were the work of God, not of men, and she wanted to make peace with Israel's God. In this, she was far wiser than the kings of Canaan.

11. THE LORD YOUR GOD, HE IS GOD IN HEAVEN ABOVE AND ON EARTH BENEATH: This is a profound confession of faith in God. Rahab helped the Jews because she recognized that their God was the one true God. This was the faith that is commended in the New Testament, and it is a testimony to God's grace that even a prostitute could be saved. God did not want to send judgment on the people of Canaan, and the tragedy of this passage is that there were so few who repented like Rahab, and so many who fought against the God of Israel to the bitter end.

12. SWEAR TO ME BY THE LORD: Rahab also recognized that there was no higher oath that God's people could swear than one sworn by His name. The spies would have brought grave dishonor upon the Lord's name if they had failed to keep their promise. Rahab already understood that the Lord was faithful to keep His promises, so she knew that an oath given in His name by His people would be binding. Later, the Lord would again honor such a promise, given by the Israelites to the people of Gibeon (Joshua 9:18), even though it would be made without consulting Him.

13. SPARE MY FATHER, MY MOTHER, MY BROTHERS, MY SISTERS: Rahab was not thinking only of herself in this time of crisis. She made it a point to also save the lives of her entire family.

THE SCARLET THREAD: *The spies instruct Rahab on how to save herself and her family from the coming destruction of Jericho—by using a scarlet thread. This thread serves to remind us of the Passover sacrifice.*

15. SHE DWELT ON THE WALL: Jericho, like other cities of the time, was surrounded by two concentric walls, the inner wall standing on higher ground than the outer one. There were houses built between those walls frequently, often with windows opening out of the walls themselves. Rahab probably dropped a rope through her window, down the front side of the outer wall, to the ground below. This was an immensely risky undertaking, as the rope and the spies would have been in plain sight, and even at night there was a great risk of being caught. The Lord was protecting His people from detection.

18. BIND THIS LINE OF SCARLET CORD IN THE WINDOW: There was a practical sense to the scarlet cord, since its color would make it easily visible against the brown mud walls of the city. But there was also an important symbolic significance in the scarlet cord, as its bloodred color pointed ahead to the final atonement of Christ. Rahab hung the cord from her window, much as the Israelites had painted their doorposts with the blood of the Passover lambs prior to leaving Egypt (Exodus 12). During the Passover, the Lord sent an angel throughout Egypt to slay the firstborn son of any household that was not covered by the blood of a sacrificed lamb. Anyone who was inside a house covered by the blood was safe from death—just as Rahab's family would only be safe if they remained inside her house when God's destruction came upon Jericho (v. 19).

By Faith: *The author of Hebrews gives many examples from the Old Testament of people who lived by faith—and Rahab is among them.*

24. By faith: Hebrews 11 is commonly referred to as the "faith chapter," because it lists many great heroes of faith from the Old Testament. The central theme of this chapter is the fact that service to God requires faith, for "without faith it is impossible to please Him, for he who comes to God must believe that He is, and that He is a rewarder of those who diligently seek Him" (v. 6). The author of Hebrews defines faith as "the substance of things hoped for, the evidence of things not seen" (v. 1). The person of faith chooses to believe in that which is "not seen" simply because God has promised that it is true.

refused to be called the son of Pharaoh's daughter: Moses had every possible blessing that this world affords, since he grew up in the royal court of the world's most powerful nation in his day. Rahab probably did not have much in terms of the world's wealth, but she did have a secure home inside the walls of a very safe and powerful city. The heroes of the faith were people who saw beyond what the world has to offer, fixing their eyes, instead, on eternity. Rahab knew that her city was doomed, simply because she believed God had the power to bring down those city walls. Like Moses, she refused to place her faith in the fortifications of mankind, choosing instead to trust in the protection and faithfulness of God.

30. By faith the walls of Jericho fell down: Rahab's faith was rewarded when God brought down the walls of Jericho—but kept her and her family completely safe. It was even the faith of the people of Israel that brought down those walls, in the sense that they obeyed God's commands to march around the city each day. It must have seemed strange to them to be marching silently around the walls, blowing rams' horns, since that is hardly a military strategy. But the Lord used their faithful obedience to work His own powerful miracle. God's people today are likewise called to live in faithful obedience.

~ Reading James 2:19–26 ~

Faith Without Works: *James tells us how to determine whether our faith is alive or dead. A living faith is demonstrated by good works.*

19. Even the demons believe: In this passage, James addressed the fact that saving faith goes beyond mere intellectual assent regarding Jesus Christ. He was not suggesting that salvation is somehow based on our works; rather, he was arguing that true faith—that which is alive and powerful—will inevitably bear fruit of repentance and righteousness in the lives of those who possess it. Faith, James said, is not a mere mental acknowledgment of the facts concerning Jesus Christ. Even the demons believe there is one God who created the heavens and the earth—but that "faith" does not save them. True saving faith, James argued, is active—being given and energized by the Holy Spirit, who transforms true believers from the inside out such that they desire to submit themselves to God and His Word. The kings of Canaan believed that Israel's God was powerful and was leading His people to victory, but that understanding did not motivate them to take the action of submitting themselves to Him. Rahab's actions, however, demonstrated that her faith was genuine—she openly forsook her former gods and embraced the Lord of creation.

20. FAITH WITHOUT WORKS IS DEAD: A faith that does not lead to repentance and obedience is a "dead faith." The faith that characterizes repentance and salvation, on the other hand, is a living faith, made evident by fruits of obedience. Though salvation is found in Christ alone by grace alone through faith alone, those who have been genuinely saved (having been transformed by the regenerating work of the Holy Spirit) will subsequently show evidence of their faith and love for God in how they live.

21. JUSTIFIED BY WORKS: Again, James was not suggesting that we gain eternal life and peace with God by doing good works or being good people. On the contrary, once we are saved and indwelt by the Holy Spirit, our faith compels us to good works. After all, our hearts and affections have been changed, such that we who were formerly enemies of God now long to please and honor Him. Abraham believed God's promises that he would have a son, and that his son would produce as many descendants as the sands of the sea. God commanded him to slay that son when he was still young, so how could God's promises come to pass? Yet Abraham's faith in God's promises gave him the ability to obey that command—and in this sense the genuineness of his faith was proven and made evident by his actions (Genesis 15:6; 22:1–18).

25. WAS NOT RAHAB THE HARLOT ALSO JUSTIFIED BY WORKS?: In the same way, Rahab had faith that God would save her and her family, and that faith led to the action of helping the spies and placing the scarlet cord in her window. The king of Jericho assented that Israel's God was mighty and faithful to His people, but his "faith" was dead—it led him to run from God and to shut up the city against Israel's approach.

﹏ First Impressions ﹏

1. *Why did the spies hide in the house of a prostitute? How was this a strategic move?*

2. *Why did Rahab help the spies? What was her motivation? What did she hope to get out of it?*

3. *Why did the spies order Rahab to bind a scarlet thread from her window? In what ways is this thread a symbol of salvation?*

4. In what ways was God's hand guiding the events in Rahab's life? What was His purpose for her? For the spies?

⌁ Some Key Principles ⌁

We are saved by faith, but that faith always leads to righteous behavior.

James drew a strong distinction between genuine saving faith and mere intellectual acceptance of God's existence. The demons themselves, he pointed out, believe in the existence of God, and they tremble at the knowledge. One might go so far as to say that the devil's understanding of God is very orthodox: he acknowledges that God is one, and that Jesus Christ is His Son who takes away the sins of the world. But that knowledge will not save the devil and his demons.

Mere knowledge about God is not enough to save a person. The person who recognizes that God exists and that He created the world does well, said James, yet even the demons exhibit that amount of faith. The faith that saves is an *active* faith, a faith that leads a person to actively repent of sin and begin to enthusiastically obey the Word of God.

A faith that does not produce fruits of righteous behavior is a dead faith, because a living faith—the kind that saves—will always lead us to obey God's Word (out of heart that has been changed and now desires to please Him). "Now by this we know that we know Him, if we keep His commandments," the apostle John wrote. "He who says, 'I know Him,' and does not keep His commandments, is a liar, and the truth is not in him. But whoever keeps His word, truly the love of God is perfected in him. By this we know that we are in Him. He who says he abides in Him ought himself also to walk just as He walked" (1 John 2:3–6).

God's grace is freely available to everyone, no matter what has happened in the past.

Rahab was a prostitute. We know nothing about her life before she met the spies, but it was obviously filled with all manner of wickedness. She was in the lowest stratum of the city, an unclean woman who lived—quite literally—on the outskirts of society. If anyone was unfit for the kingdom of God, it was Rahab. Yet God redeemed her—more than that, He elevated her from the dregs of society to the highest of honors: her descendants culminated in the person of Jesus Christ.

Everyone has sinned and fallen short of the glory of God (Romans 3:23), and one sin is just as grievous as another in God's eyes. The prostitute is no more unfit for God's kingdom than the law-abiding citizen: all people are equally in need of God's forgiveness and grace. That's the bad news; the good news is that God has made forgiveness available to everyone who will believe in Him—to the grossest of sinners as well as the person who has lived a "good life."

And the best news is that God's grace is *freely* available; there is nothing that anyone can do to earn it or deserve it. Rahab did not deserve to be saved. Yet God, in His grace, chose to rescue her and her family from certain destruction. Similarly, through the Cross, God has made eternal salvation available to sinners who do not deserve it. He offers it freely to all who would repent of their sins and embrace in faith His Son, Jesus Christ.

God transforms sinners into saints.

As we've already said, Rahab was a grievous sinner, someone who had deliberately disobeyed God's commands for a righteous life. Saving her from judgment would have been a tremendous act of grace all by itself, but God did far more than that: He transformed her into a woman of God, and she was ultimately in the lineage of Christ.

Saul of Tarsus was also a grievous sinner. He spent his adult life persecuting the early Christian church, hunting down and arresting anyone who professed faith in Jesus. He was even instrumental in putting Christians to death, assisting those who stoned them. Yet God saved him, gave him the name *Paul*, and transformed him into an apostle whose writings fill the New Testament.

Our salvation is merely the first step in God's amazing work of redemption. The person who repents of sin and embraces God's grace through faith in Jesus Christ receives the inestimable gift of eternal life—and he also receives the gift of the Holy Spirit. The Spirit immediately begins the work of transformation in our lives, gradually making us more like Jesus Christ. This is the ultimate act of transformation, exceeding even that of Rahab: the lowliest of sinners will one day reflect the full glory of God's Son, Jesus!

⤚ Digging Deeper ⤙

5. Was it right, wrong, or indifferent for Rahab to lie about the spies? How might she have handled the situation without lying?

6. What exactly is faith? Why is faith necessary if we are to please God?

7. What is the difference between a living faith and a dead faith? How did Rahab demonstrate a living faith? How did the king of Jericho (or the king of Jerusalem from Study 3) demonstrate a dead faith?

8. *Have you accepted God's free gift of salvation by placing your faith in His Son, Jesus Christ? If not, what is preventing you from doing so now?*

⌁ Taking It Personally ⌁

9. *In what ways has the Lord transformed your life since you became a Christian? What transformations is He working on at present?*

10. *Is your faith a living one? Are you walking in obedience to God's Word? What areas of obedience might the Lord be calling you to work on this week?*

~ 7 ~
DEBORAH AND BARAK

✧ HISTORICAL BACKGROUND ✧

Prior to the events in this study, Joshua had led the Israelites to a great victory over an alliance of kingdoms that had mobilized specifically to fight against Israel (see Joshua 11). This enemy federation was led by Jabin, king of Hazor. The name *Jabin* was probably a title rather than a personal name, similar to the title *Pharaoh* in Egypt, since we now find another Jabin in Hazor, hundreds of years later—and once again raising an army to fight against God's people.

This event took place during the time of the judges, and our focus is on the northern tribes of Israel near Dan. (See the map in the Introduction.) "Jabin" had risen to power once again, and he had drawn together a coalition of smaller cities with a powerful army. This army was equipped with a huge force of chariots—iron chariots. Iron was a relatively new invention at this time, and it was vastly superior to the bronze it replaced. Iron was used not only for swords but also for armor, both for soldiers and for their chariots, lending formidable strength to a cavalry unit. Israel, however, did not have any iron weapons or armor, and certainly no iron-clad chariots. They were outnumbered and outclassed by the mighty army of Jabin.

Jabin's military advantages gave him the ability to oppress the people of Israel, and he took full advantage of it for twenty years. We do not know the details of his oppression, but it probably involved huge tax burdens for the Israelites, as well as oppressive laws restricting their freedoms. The Philistines, for example, made it illegal for Israel to work with iron, so their weapons would remain inferior.

The northern tribes of Israel were being led at this time by a judge named Deborah, referred to as "a mother in Israel" (Judges 5:7). She was a woman of wisdom and prudence, and the people of Israel came to her for judgment when settling civil disagreements. The fighting men of Israel were led by Barak, about whom little is known. Barak was probably a man of courage and fighting skill, since he had risen to a position of leadership, but in this study we will discover that even a seasoned fighter can succumb to the sin of fear.

⌒ READING JUDGES 4:1–24 ⌒

GOD RAISES UP DEBORAH: *Israel's repeated disobedience leads the Lord to raise up an enemy for discipline. But soon He also raises up a judge to deliver them—Deborah.*

1. EHUD: One of the so-called major judges of Israel (Judges 3).

THE CHILDREN OF ISRAEL AGAIN DID EVIL IN THE SIGHT OF THE LORD: This is a constant refrain in the book of Judges. The Israelites would fall into wickedness; then the Lord would deliver them into suffering, usually at the hands of the Canaanite nations that the people had failed to drive out; the people would then raise their voices in suffering to the Lord; the Lord would respond by raising up a judge to deliver them—then repeat. This is not the way God wants to interact with His people. He calls us to obey Him with willing hearts, rather than to live in an endless cycle of sin and discipline.

2. HAZOR: Located just south of Dan. See the map in the Introduction.

THE COMMANDER OF HIS ARMY WAS SISERA: The general of Jabin's army.

4. DEBORAH . . . WAS JUDGING ISRAEL AT THAT TIME: Deborah was the only woman listed in the Old Testament as a judge in Israel. Indeed, female leadership among God's people was exceedingly rare in Israel. In the New Testament, the principle that the Lord has laid down for the church is that men are called to lead.

5. THE CHILDREN OF ISRAEL CAME UP TO HER FOR JUDGMENT: Not all of Israel's judges are said to have "held court" to settle disputes and legal matters, although there were others who did so besides Deborah. Her role as arbiter suggests that she had great wisdom. Her name means "bee," and she probably had many beelike qualities: industry, diligence, and prudence, for example.

7. AGAINST YOU I WILL DEPLOY SISERA: This is an interesting picture of God's sovereignty over human affairs. It suggests that the Lord was going to act as the commander of the enemy's army, deploying them as He saw fit. This is similar to the way the Lord hardened the heart of Pharaoh before the Exodus: Pharaoh had *already* set his heart firmly against God and His people, so the Lord used his hardness of heart to accomplish His own purposes. In the same way, the Lord here was promising that He would turn Sisera's aggression against himself, leading his army into Israel's hands.

BARAK'S UNWILLING LEADERSHIP: *The Lord commands Barak to lead His people to victory, but he is afraid to obey. He makes a counteroffer, depriving himself of blessing.*

8. IF YOU WILL NOT GO WITH ME, I WILL NOT GO: Barak's response was not pleasing to the Lord, both because it was disobedient and because it demonstrated a lack of faith. The Lord had commanded him to lead the army into battle, and there was no room for negotiations. A military leader does not make bargains with his commanders; he simply obeys his orders. Barak, however, tried to make stipulations on obedience because he did not fully believe that the Lord would keep His promise of victory. He needed some form of security to ensure that the Lord would keep His word, and this lack of faith demonstrated that he did not fully trust in the character of God.

9. THE LORD WILL SELL SISERA INTO THE HAND OF A WOMAN: This woman would turn out to be Jael, not Deborah. For Barak's victory to be ascribed to a woman would have been a disgrace, for it was a man's part to lead an army into battle.

10. ZEBULUN AND NAPHTALI: Two tribes of Israel.

11. THE FATHER-IN-LAW OF MOSES: The Kenites were distantly related to the Israelites and had a strong tradition of cooperation and peace with God's people. It was no accident that this man and his family were living near Jabin; the Lord intended to use them to accomplish His purposes.

13. CHARIOTS OF IRON: This was the dawn of the so-called Iron Age, when iron was a relatively new invention. It was so far superior to bronze for weaponry that the Philistines would not allow the Israelites to make it. The armies of Israel, in fact, were generally underequipped in all respects, including their weapons and armor. The prospect of facing a chariot of iron would have been comparable to facing a modern-day tank.

17. SISERA HAD FLED AWAY: The army of Israel had routed Sisera's forces, but their leader had escaped. This would have been an inconclusive victory at best if Sisera had survived, since he might then have raised another army and attacked Israel again. If Barak had not balked at the Lord's command, God would have delivered Sisera into his hand during the battle. But he did not obey completely, so the Lord reserved Sisera for the hand of a woman.

JAEL GAINS THE VICTORY: *Barak had refused to lead the army of Israel, so the Lord gave the victory to an unknown woman.*

THERE WAS PEACE BETWEEN JABIN ... AND THE HOUSE OF HEBER: The Kenites were noted metalworkers, and it is possible that Heber had made peace with Jabin in order to work on his iron chariots.

18. JAEL WENT OUT TO MEET SISERA: It is probable that Jael was concerned about the outcome of the battle that day, since she had divided loyalties. Her family was at peace with Jabin, yet her clan was at peace with Israel. In this fatal encounter, Jael showed where her true allegiance lay.

INTO THE TENT: It was a severe breach of etiquette for a man other than her husband to enter a woman's tent. Sisera was probably desperate at this moment, willing to hide himself under the protective skirts of a woman in order to save himself. This attitude was similar to Barak's, in that Barak was afraid to go into battle without Deborah by his side.

19. SHE OPENED A JUG OF MILK: Sisera requested water, but Jael gave him milk. Milk is not a good thirst quencher on a hot day, especially after a man has undergone the physical exertions of battle and flight. It is possible that Jael wanted to make Sisera sleepy so that she could carry out her own plan.

21. TOOK A TENT PEG AND . . . A HAMMER: The hammer and tent pegs were used to keep the tents secure. It was a woman's work to set up and take down the tents, so Jael would have been well familiar with their use.

DROVE THE PEG INTO HIS TEMPLE: Ordinarily, the laws of hospitality would have required that a guest be protected and cared for while in a person's tent. But Jael's loyalties lay with the people of Israel, and she understood that she would be helping God's enemies if she harbored Sisera. She was faced with a difficult decision, but she did not hesitate to obey the Lord's command to destroy Sisera and his forces. Once again, she provided a stark contrast to Barak.

⌢ READING JUDGES 5:1–31 ⌢

THE SONG OF DEBORAH: *Deborah and Barak sing of Israel's victory, and of the Lord's great faithfulness to His people.*

5:1. DEBORAH AND BARAK . . . SANG ON THAT DAY: There has been some conjecture over the authorship of this memorable poem, but it seems most likely that it was written by Deborah. The verb *sang* is in the feminine singular, implying that Barak was joining Deborah in a song that she had written.

2. WHEN LEADERS LEAD IN ISRAEL: This concept is important in understanding the period of the judges. There were numerous times when God's chosen leaders were hesitant to take the lead, as we will see again in Gideon's life. Barak refused to take the full responsibility to which the Lord had called him, and as a result, he lost much of the reward that might have been his.

WHEN THE PEOPLE WILLINGLY OFFER THEMSELVES: Notice that there are two parts to receiving the Lord's full blessing here: the leaders must lead, and the people must willingly follow. The people of Israel frequently rejected the authority of those whom the Lord placed over them, such as Moses, and at such times He sent discipline upon them. God's people would be richly blessed if the leaders would lead (according to God's instructions) and the people would follow.

7. Until I, Deborah, arose: Compare Judges 4:6–9. The Lord had called Barak to lead the people out of bondage to their enemies, but his refusal meant that the credit for the victory would go to a woman. Jael received most of the recognition by defeating Sisera, but here we see that Deborah ultimately was credited with the spiritual leadership in Israel.

9. the rulers of Israel who offered themselves willingly: Deborah again underscored the importance of leaders who are willing to sacrifice themselves in service to God's people. Note the repetition of the idea of willingness, both in leading and in following. The Lord calls His people to obey with willing hearts, rather than grudging spirits.

11. they shall recount the righteous acts of the Lord: The victory over Israel's enemies ultimately belonged to the Lord, rather than to the deeds of men. God demonstrated His faithfulness by bringing about a great victory over Sisera's army, despite the fact that some of His people did not willingly do what they were told.

17. Gilead stayed beyond the Jordan: Some of the tribes of Israel had failed to come to the aid of their brethren in this battle. Their absence was noticed, despite the fact that the Lord brought a great victory without them.

18. who jeopardized their lives to the point of death: Conversely, those who fought at their own peril were remembered and honored for their faithfulness to God's people. Those who faithfully participate in the Lord's work will be blessed, while those who shirk their responsibilities will deprive themselves of reward.

20. They fought from the heavens: Deborah recognized that the victory came from the Lord, not from Israel's military might.

28. The mother of Sisera: It is interesting that the principal characters mentioned in Deborah's song are women—on both sides of the conflict. Note that the song rarely mentions any deeds on the part of Barak.

⌁ First Impressions ⌁

1. *In what ways did Sisera's army have the advantage over the army of Israel? How would you have felt if you were in Israel's army? In Sisera's army?*

2. *How might the outcome of the battle have been different if Barak had fully obeyed God's command?*

3. *In your opinion, was Jael justified in what she did to Sisera? Why or why not?*

4. *Why did God deliver Sisera into the hands of Jael? What was wrong with Barak's request to have Deborah join him in leadership?*

↜ Some Key Principles ↜

Be strong and courageous.

We have considered this principle in a previous study, but it is worth reiterating here. The Lord commanded Barak to lead His people into battle, and He even promised that the Israelites would see a great victory. The Lord had made such promises many times before, and He had never failed to keep those promises. Yet Barak was hesitant to obey.

We are not told what motivated his hesitancy. Perhaps he felt unqualified to lead the army or thought that Deborah had a better "connection" with the mind of God than he did. Or maybe he was just afraid. Whatever his motivation, fear was the foundation. He was afraid he would fail—or more accurately, he was afraid that God would fail, that His promises would not come to pass.

While at times, fear can motivate a person to take action in a dangerous situation, in the long run it cripples rather than energizes. Fear is based on a lack of trust in God's character, a core belief that He will not keep His promises. Courage is just the opposite— it motivates a Christian to move forward in faith, despite the appearance of circumstances. Courage is based on faith in God's character, a firm belief that He is always faithful. Courage brings freedom and victory, while fear brings bondage and failure.

God calls men to take the lead in the church and home.

The Lord called Barak to lead His army into battle, and his hesitancy caused him to lose credit for the great victory that followed. The credit went instead to a woman, which was considered a great disgrace in the social milieu of the ancient Middle East.

Our culture today would not consider it a disgrace for a woman to receive the accolades for such a victory, and we are accustomed to women in all spheres of leadership. It is easy for God's people to assume that the world's ideas of "egalitarianism" apply to the church as well—in fact, the world condemns those who suggest that there are some roles to which women are not called. Yet that is the case in God's definition for the church and home: men are called to take the lead, and women are called to submit to their leadership.

The flip side to this is just as important to understand: if men want women to follow, they must be willing to take the lead. If Barak thought it was a disgrace to lose the credit to a woman, then he should have been willing to take the lead in the first place. When men refuse to stand up and lead in the church or home, they must expect that women will fill the void.

Christians are to obey God's commands, not to negotiate for a "better deal."

Barak was the leader of Israel's military, and as such he was probably accustomed to having his commands obeyed without argument. After all, a good soldier never talks back to a commanding officer; he carries out commands without comment. It was all the more startling, therefore, when Barak countermanded the direct orders of his Commanding Officer—God Himself.

Picture a general commanding a soldier to move into battle, and the soldier responds, "I will go into battle as long as you come with me; if you won't come with me, then I won't go." That soldier's career would be short. Yet how much more audacious is it when a believer tries to find ways around simple obedience to God's Word! We do this when we obey only part way, or tell ourselves that we will begin to obey tomorrow, or when we ignore the Holy Spirit's promptings.

The Lord wants His people to obey His Word, and to obey eagerly—not by compulsion. We cannot experience the Lord's full blessing in our lives unless we willingly obey His commands. As Deborah sang, "When leaders lead in Israel, when the people willingly offer themselves, bless the LORD!" (Judges 5:2).

⌁ DIGGING DEEPER ⌁

5. *What evidence do you see in the battle against Sisera of God's sovereign leadership? How did the Lord arrange events for Israel's victory?*

6. *Why do you think Barak hesitated to lead the army into battle? Why did he demand that Deborah go with him?*

7. What examples of courage do you find in these passages? What examples do you find of fear? What resulted from each?

8. Are you a willing leader? A willing follower? Are there some areas where God has to coerce you into obedience?

9. Are you facing life's challenges with courage or with fear? How can you increase your courage in the coming days and weeks?

10. Are you presently trying to negotiate with God? In what areas of your life is He calling you to increased obedience?

~ 8 ~
GIDEON

⌁ HISTORICAL BACKGROUND ⌁

In our studies so far, we have seen numerous instances when foreign armies came against Israel in open battle. But open warfare was not the only threat Israel faced; there were also times when the nation's enemies used tactics similar to those of the terrorists of today—sweeping into the land and quickly out again, destroying crops and cattle and people along the way. That was the situation at the time of Gideon, another of Israel's judges.

As we have discovered from previous studies, this situation arose because the people of Israel had wandered away from the Lord and embraced instead the pagan practices of the world around them. Once again, the people had repented under the oppression of their enemies, and again the Lord raised up a judge to lead them out of bondage. This time, however, we will discover that the judge himself allowed paganism to enter his own home. (We will see this trend even more dramatically in our study on Samson.)

Gideon was evidently from a fairly wealthy family, and he had lived his life tending crops and herds. Israel's enemies at that time were raiding the land and causing such devastation that even a well-off man like Gideon barely had enough food. We meet Gideon as he is skulking about, trying to thresh wheat in secret and hoping that his enemies will not swoop in and kill him in the process.

The Lord came to Gideon in human form and greeted him as a "man of valor." At first glance, this seems incongruous, since Gideon was trying to stay out of sight and avoid any open confrontation. But the Lord had great plans for him, because He saw beyond Gideon's timidity and fears. Even so, it will take some time for Gideon to live up to that badge of honor, as he continued to demonstrate his fear by putting the Lord's promises to the test.

ᴧ Reading Judges 6:1–40 ᴧ

Like a Plague of Locusts: *The nation of Israel continues the cycle of sin and repentance, and this time the Lord sends marauding Midianites to discipline His people.*

1. THE CHILDREN OF ISRAEL DID EVIL IN THE SIGHT OF THE LORD: Here once again we see the old cycle of sin, discipline, and repentance that characterized the nation of Israel during the times of the judges. This time, the Lord put them under the oppression of the Midianites, a nation of wandering herdsmen who lived east of the Red Sea. They were distant relations of Israel, descended from Abraham and his second wife, Keturah, whom he married after the death of Sarah (Genesis 25:1–2). Israel had a long and unpleasant history with Midian—it was a group of Midianite merchants who bought Joseph from his brothers and carried him into slavery in Egypt (Genesis 37:28), and it was also the Midianites who hired Balaam to curse Israel (Numbers 22:7).

2. THE DENS, THE CAVES, AND THE STRONGHOLDS: The Midianites' oppression over Israel was more than mere dictatorship, such as that which they had experienced under Jabin (see Study 7). The Midianites were raiding and plundering and murdering the people, and the Israelites were forced to flee for their very lives.

5. AS NUMEROUS AS LOCUSTS: A swarm of locusts can sweep across a field and leave it completely stripped of grain with the suddenness and fury of a passing storm. The use of this phrase here vividly depicts the absolute devastation that the Midianites and their allies were wreaking on Israel's crops.

THEIR CAMELS: This is the first reference in Scripture of camels used in warfare. The camel was first tamed and used in domestic and military functions during the Iron Age, and it is quite possible that Israel had never encountered it in battle before this. The camel could travel great distances in short amounts of time, making it an early example of a long-range military weapon.

Raising Gideon: *The people cry out to the Lord, and He raises up Gideon to lead them against the Midianites.*

6. THE CHILDREN OF ISRAEL CRIED OUT TO THE LORD: The cycle of sin and repentance was being replayed here yet again, but on this occasion the Lord's response would be different from the past.

10. YOU HAVE NOT OBEYED MY VOICE: On this occasion, the Lord sent a prophet to Israel to rebuke the people for their constant cycle of sin and disobedience. He reminded them of all that He had done in the past, bringing them out of slavery in Egypt and giving them one miraculous victory after another over the people of Canaan. Yet the people had responded to God's great faithfulness by being unfaithful in return. They had begun to embrace the idolatrous practices of the world around them. The people were testing the Lord's patience in their sin-and-repentance cycle, and He warned them that He would not endure their hard-heartedness indefinitely.

11. THE ANGEL OF THE LORD: Here we have another theophany, the Lord Himself appearing in human form.

GIDEON THRESHED WHEAT IN THE WINEPRESS: Wheat was ordinarily threshed on a large wooden floor that was open on all sides, permitting the wind to carry away the chaff. Grapes, on the other hand, were pressed in small pits carved into rock, so this suggests that Gideon did not have much wheat to thresh in the first place. It also shows how much the people of Israel lived in dread of the Midianite raiders—they were afraid to be seen with the smallest quantity of food.

12. YOU MIGHTY MAN OF VALOR: This greeting may seem ironic at first, since Gideon was anything but a man of courage at this point, hiding away under a tree to keep his grain out of view. But the Lord was not looking at what he was; He was interested in what Gideon would become under His transforming hand.

13. THE LORD HAS FORSAKEN US: Gideon obviously had an imperfect understanding of God's character. He accused the Lord of having forsaken His people, in spite of God's reiterated promise that He would never do so (Deuteronomy 4:31). His question of why the Lord had delivered Israel into the hands of Midian indicated that he also failed to recognize the sinful and disobedient condition of his nation.

14. THE LORD TURNED TO HIM: God turned His face upon Gideon, showing him great favor and honor. In that moment, evidently, Gideon's eyes were opened, and he realized that he was in the presence of the Lord.

GO IN THIS MIGHT OF YOURS: The Lord had just told Gideon that He was with him, and that He would cause him to become a "mighty man of valor" (v. 12), but Gideon had remained in doubt. Here God was encouraging Gideon to step out in faith, trusting that the Lord had given him a new level of strength and courage. These gifts would ultimately be from the Lord, but to receive them, Gideon must first take action.

GIDEON'S DOUBTS: *The Lord commands Gideon to be a man of valor, but Gideon responds with doubts and fears.*

15. HOW CAN I SAVE ISRAEL?: On one hand, it is understandable that Gideon reacted this way. He was a humble man, recognizing his own weaknesses and shortcomings. Moses responded in a similar manner at the burning bush (Exodus 3). Yet the Lord's response was the same to both Gideon and Moses: "You can do what I am commanding, because I will be with you, and I shall enable you to accomplish it." Gideon's doubts at this point arose because he did not trust the Lord to fight the battle for him; he envisioned himself fighting the battle in his own strength. The principle is the same for Christians today: the Lord gives us the power needed to carry out His commands.

17. SHOW ME A SIGN: On the surface, it might almost seem reasonable for Gideon to make these requests to the Lord. After all, it was very unusual for the Lord to appear to a man, and the command He was giving was potentially disastrous for all of Gideon's people if it turned out to not be from God. But in the long run, it will become apparent that Gideon was merely stalling, hoping to find a way around simple obedience to the Lord.

18. DO NOT DEPART FROM HERE: This scene was repeated in almost every detail many years later, when the angel of the Lord appeared to the parents of Samson.

19. UNLEAVENED BREAD FROM AN EPHAH OF FLOUR: Gideon prepared a sacrificial offering for the Lord. It was also a very generous offering—especially in a time of famine—since an ephah was approximately twenty pounds of flour.

22. I HAVE SEEN THE ANGEL OF THE LORD FACE TO FACE: Gideon was filled with fear because he realized that he had been speaking with the Lord Himself, in person—and he knew that the Lord had once told Moses, "You cannot see My face; for no man shall see Me, and live" (Exodus 33:20). Yet even in this response, Gideon demonstrated his lack of understanding concerning God's character. The Lord had appeared to him specifically to promise that He would not destroy him, but rather be with him and give him great victory.

GIDEON'S FIRST ASSIGNMENT: *Before he can lead the people into battle against Midian, Gideon must first cleanse his own house of idolatry.*

25. TEAR DOWN THE ALTAR OF BAAL . . . AND CUT DOWN THE WOODEN IMAGE: This command gives us insight into the spiritual condition of Israel in Gideon's time. His own father had built an altar to a pagan god, and was evidently offering sacrifices to Baal. The wooden image was probably a pole set up in honor of the pagan goddess Asherah, a very common element of idolatry in Canaan at the time. The Lord had expressly forbidden His people to engage in such idolatrous practices, and He had further commanded His people to destroy the pagan altars of those already living in Canaan (Exodus 34:13)—yet they had gone so far into disobedience as to build altars of their own.

26. BUILD AN ALTAR TO THE LORD YOUR GOD: This seems to suggest that Gideon did not have an altar for the Lord, or at least not one that was constructed "in the proper arrangement" (Exodus 20:25). It is significant that the Lord commanded Gideon to get his own house in order before leading Israel in battle against Midian. The Lord calls His people to the same priorities today: we must cleanse our own lives of idolatry and disobedience before we can be effective in bringing the gospel to others.

SNEAKING AROUND AT NIGHT: *Gideon obeys the Lord's commands to tear down his father's pagan shrine—but he does it under cover of darkness because he is afraid.*

27. HE DID IT BY NIGHT: Gideon finally demonstrated the true motive for his previous hesitations: fear. As we have seen repeatedly in these studies, fear leads people away from God, not toward Him. Gideon feared his neighbors more than he trusted God's faithfulness—the Lord had promised him great victory over his enemies, but he was afraid of offending the people next door. Nevertheless, despite his overwhelming trepidation, Gideon still obeyed.

30. BRING OUT YOUR SON: This suggests that Gideon went into hiding after obeying the Lord's command. The people's response did lend some credence to Gideon's fears, as they were so outraged that they demanded his death. The dreadful irony was that it was the people of the city who deserved to be stoned to death for their unfaithfulness and idolatry (Deuteronomy 13:6–10).

31. JOASH SAID TO ALL WHO STOOD AGAINST HIM: It is rather sad that Joash the idolater had more courage than Gideon, the one called by God. But the Lord was not finished with Gideon; He would eventually make him into a man of courage, as He prophesied in their first meeting.

32. JERUBBAAL: Literally, "Let Baal plead." Joash gave his son this nickname in derision of the Canaanite idolaters, who prayed to a nonexistent god who could not even defend his own altar—never mind care for the people who prayed there.

34. THE SPIRIT OF THE LORD CAME UPON GIDEON: This powerful phrase literally means that the Spirit of the Lord clothed Gideon. It suggests that God Himself took control of the ensuing battle, fighting on behalf of His people.

FLEECING GOD: *Even after the victory over his idolatrous neighbors, Gideon is still afraid. The Lord has told him what to do, but he seeks further proof that God will be faithful.*

36. IF YOU WILL SAVE ISRAEL BY MY HAND: In spite of the powerful presence of the Holy Spirit, Gideon was still fearful. He was still struggling to believe that God would keep His promise and bring about a great victory.

37. I shall put a fleece of wool: To this day, people sometimes speak about "putting out a fleece" to gain guidance from the Lord. It is important to understand, however, that Gideon's actions were motivated by a lack of faith, not by a desire to seek wise counsel. The Lord did not reprimand Gideon for his uncertainty—in fact, He graciously granted him the reassurance that he sought—yet this approach to God's commands is not a model for us to follow.

39. Let me test: Gideon himself recognized that his fleece tests were not in accordance with God's will—note that he asked the Lord to not become angry with him. God had commanded His people to not put Him to the test (see Deuteronomy 6:16; the word translated "tempt" is the same as "test" here), yet Gideon was doing just that—testing the Lord to see whether He would and could keep His promises. Nevertheless, the Lord demonstrated His great grace and patience by performing what Gideon requested.

⌒ First Impressions ⌒

1. When have you been faced with an enemy or a situation that overwhelmed you? How did you respond? How would you respond now if you were to face those same circumstances again?

2. Why did Gideon ask for signs from God? What did this reveal about his faith? About God's character?

3. *Why did the Lord command Gideon to destroy his father's pagan altar? Why was this impor-*
   tant to do first before fighting the Midianites?

4. *Why did Gideon destroy the altar at night? What was the result of his obedience?*

⌒ Some Key Principles ⌒

Ask God for guidance, but don't put Him to the test.

The Scriptures abound with men and women who were faced with difficult circumstances or decisions, and they turned to the Lord for guidance. Jesus urged His disciples
to seek the Father's will in all things, teaching them to pray, "Your will be done on earth
as it is in heaven" (Matthew 6:10). Today, Christians receive the indwelling of the Holy
Spirit, whose role in part is to guide us into all truth (John 16:13). There is no need to
"test" God in order to receive direction.

Yet it is also important to recognize that this was not what Gideon was really doing
when he put out his fleeces. The Lord had already given him guidance, telling him exactly
what he was to do—but Gideon was afraid. He feared that the Lord would not keep
His promises, and he sought miraculous verification of God's faithfulness. The Lord
had repeatedly proven Himself faithful throughout Israel's history—parting the Jordan

River for them to cross, bringing down the walls of Jericho, giving His people one victory after another against powerful enemies—and Gideon should have rested in faith that the Lord would keep His word once again.

Modern Christians also have a record of God's faithfulness through the ages. We learn of it throughout the Bible, as we read the testimonies of those who have walked with Him in the past. If we live in light of God's Word, obeying the truth that He has revealed to us in Scripture, we can do so with confidence—knowing that God will be faithful in the present just as He has been in the past.

Do not fear what man may do.

Gideon lived in terrifying times. His nation was under such oppression and persecution that they did not have enough food to eat, and they were in constant fear for their lives. From a human perspective, it is easy to understand why Gideon would have been afraid to go into battle against Israel's powerful enemies, or even to take a bold stand against the idolatry of his family and neighbors. After all, he was not a trained soldier and evidently had lived his life looking after the family's crops and herds.

Interestingly, David had a similar background and faced a comparable situation—yet his response to the Lord's commands was vastly different from Gideon's. David, the youthful shepherd with no military experience, boldly confronted the giant Goliath, the Philistine army's most seasoned champion. Both David and Gideon faced terrifying foes, but it was the Lord who fought the battles in both cases.

David wrote, "I called on the LORD in distress; the LORD answered me and set me in a broad place. The LORD is on my side; I will not fear. What can man do to me?" (Psalm 118:5–6). And Hebrews 13:5–6 tells us, "[God] Himself has said, 'I will never leave you nor forsake you.' So we may boldly say: 'The LORD is my helper; I will not fear. What can man do to me?'"

The spiritual battle begins at home.

The people of Israel had cried out to God for deliverance from their deadly enemies, so the Lord raised up Gideon to drive out the marauders from Midian. And God eventually brought about a great victory for Israel's forces under Gideon's leadership, but first Gideon needed to address the idolatry in his own home. The Lord commanded him to begin by tearing down his father's pagan altar and replacing it with a proper altar at which to worship the God of Israel.

This small battle on the home front was important for Gideon in several ways. It gave him a taste of battle and taught him that he could trust the Lord. It increased his boldness in obeying the Lord's commands and taught him that he didn't need to fear the unrighteous wrath of his neighbors. Most important, it put him in right relationship with God as he removed the idols from his own house and set up a proper place of worship.

The same principle applies today to God's people. We are called to be salt and light in the world, a living testimony to the truth of the gospel. But our testimony cannot be effective if we are not living in obedience to God's Word—sinful habits and open disobedience dim our light and make our salt lose its savor. "You are the salt of the earth," Jesus told us, "but if the salt loses its flavor, how shall it be seasoned? It is then good for nothing but to be thrown out and trampled underfoot by men" (Matthew 5:13).

ᚼ DIGGING DEEPER ᚼ

5. *Why did the Lord send a prophet to the people of Israel before raising up Gideon to defeat the Midianites? What does this suggest about the Lord's patience with persistent sin?*

6. *Why did God refer to Gideon as a "mighty man of valor"? How would you have described him at that point in his life?*

7. *What is the difference between asking God for guidance and putting Him to the test?*

8. What seemed to be Gideon's greatest concern in this passage? How might his life have been different if he had trusted the Lord more?

↶ Taking It Personally ↷

9. In what areas are you currently seeking God's wisdom for decisions you are facing? How are you applying biblical principles to those decisions? Are you eagerly following those principles, or do you find yourself putting God's Word to the test?

10. Do you tend to fear what people will say or do if you openly obey the Lord's commands? How can you increase your faith and trust in God this week?

~ 9 ~
SAMSON

↳ HISTORICAL BACKGROUND ↰

The Philistines were a seafaring people who had probably moved into Canaan from the Greek islands over a long period of time. Today we use the term *philistine* to refer to someone who is uncouth or barbaric, but that term does not describe the people who lived during the time of the judges. On the contrary, they were a very wealthy and powerful civilization, and their armies were feared around the world. Even the great Egypt could not defeat them.

Our passage for this study opens at a time when the Philistines had become the overlords of the nation of Israel. Their rule over Israel was not tyrannical in the sense of harsh laws and punishments or enslavement. Instead, the Philistines ruled by economic means, imposing taxes and a few laws on the people while still permitting them to live with some measure of autonomy. The people of Israel were kept on a leash, but it was a golden leash. In fact, the Israelites experienced a measure of comfort and economic wealth during this time, and it was an easy yoke to bear.

That was part of the problem that threatened God's people: they were becoming too comfortable under the dominion of their heathen neighbors. They were slipping into a state of spiritual lethargy and were in danger of becoming just one more pagan nation in Canaan. As we saw in our study of Gideon, the people of Israel were gradually embracing the pagan practices of the world around them, and the Lord would not tolerate such apostasy from His people.

So God raised up yet another judge to lead His people, but this time His plan was not to defeat the enemy in one open battle. Instead, He used His judge to stir up trouble between Israel and the Philistines, waking His people up from their spiritual stupor and forcing them to recognize their grave danger. This was to be the calling of Samson, a man set apart for God even before his birth. The Lord appeared to Samson's parents before he was born, instructing them to raise him as a Nazirite—a man who takes a vow of purity, made evident to the world by his abstinence from wine, avoiding dead bodies, and never cutting his hair. Samson was called to a life of purity and power; but he did not live up to that calling.

⌒ READING JUDGES 15:9–20 ⌒

THE PHILISTINES' REVENGE: *Samson has attacked the Philistines, and then gone off to a cave. The Philistines come looking for revenge.*

9. THE PHILISTINES: The Lord had allowed His people to become subject to the Philistines in their continuing cycle of sin, judgment, and repentance. Contrary to the popular image, the Philistines were a very advanced and powerful people. They were world renowned for their fine pottery, and they were feared in Canaan for their formidable military forces. Their nation comprised five major city-states: Gath, Ashkelon, Ashdod, Ekron, and Gaza. The modern-day Gaza strip is built on the Philistine city.

LEHI: Meaning "jawbone." The exact location is not known, but it probably received this name after Samson's great slaughter there.

10. SAMSON: The Lord had appeared to Samson's parents before he was born, prophesying that their son would one day deliver God's people from the Philistine oppression. They were given strict instructions, however, that he was to live under the strictures of the Nazirite vow. Samson was forbidden by God to drink wine, to touch any dead body, or to cut his hair. By the time our passage begins, however, he had grown to manhood—and had already violated two of the three stipulations by getting drunk and touching a lion's carcass. See Judges 13–14 for the full story.

AS HE HAS DONE TO US: Samson had murdered a number of Philistines in order to pay off a bet, and had subsequently burned Philistine crops and slaughtered a great many more people (Judges 14:1–15:8).

BINDING THE STRONG MAN: *The men of Judah simply want to live in peace with the Philistines—even if it means betraying their own judge to maintain that peace.*

11. THREE THOUSAND MEN OF JUDAH: This was an amazingly strong response to the situation, and it indicates that Samson's terrible strength was already well known. The response of so many men of Judah also suggests that they had grown quite comfortable under the oppression of the Philistines. Their question, "Do you not know that the Philistines rule over us?" indicates that they were content to leave things as they were. But that was not the Lord's plan for His people, and for that reason He raised up a judge who could begin the overthrow of the Philistines single-handedly.

AS THEY DID TO ME, SO I HAVE DONE TO THEM: There is ample room for doubt about the accuracy of this statement. The Philistines had cheated Samson at his own wedding feast, and his father-in-law had given his bride to another man after Samson disappeared for a period of time. Yet Samson's actions had been excessive and bloody: he had lost a bet for thirty changes of clothes and had collected the payment from the bodies of thirty murdered people from another Philistine city. He had then slaughtered many more Philistines and had burned their crops in retaliation for losing his wife to another man. The Lord was using Samson's actions to move the Israelites out of their complacency under Philistine rule, yet Samson's life was no model of godliness.

12. THAT WE MAY DELIVER YOU INTO THE HAND OF THE PHILISTINES: The men of Judah were guilty of treachery in this action. They should have banded together under the leadership of God's chosen judge and fought against the Philistines, rather than cooperating with them to deliver one of their own people up to the oppressor. This further demonstrates that the people of Israel were growing dangerously complacent, content to follow the world around them rather than to obey God's commands.

13. TWO NEW ROPES: New ropes would have been stronger and more reliable than ropes that had been used before. The fact that they used two ropes suggests that Samson's arms were bound tightly to his side, the ropes twining about his torso and possibly even constricting his legs. The men of Judah were not taking chances, yet their confidence was placed in the wrong direction—they trusted two little ropes rather than God.

GOD'S POWER UNLEASHED: *The Spirit of the Lord comes upon Samson, and he is transformed into a superhuman fighter. No army can stand before him.*

14. THE SPIRIT OF THE LORD CAME MIGHTILY UPON HIM: We saw this same phenomenon in the life of Gideon (Judges 6:34), and it was repeated in the lives of many of the judges. The Lord's Spirit manifested His power in a unique way in Samson's life, however, giving him superhuman physical strength. The anointing of the Holy Spirit was very rare prior to the ascension of Christ. The Spirit came upon men temporarily, enabling them to accomplish something beyond their human powers, but did not necessarily remain with them indefinitely. This is one of the many great gifts the Lord has provided to His children today, through Christ: that Christians are permanently indwelt by the person of God's Holy Spirit.

LIKE FLAX THAT IS BURNED WITH FIRE: The two new ropes proved laughable when the Spirit came upon Samson. The men of Judah may not have recognized that it was the power of God, not the power of a man, that was filling Samson—for binding the Holy Spirit with rope is like trying to stop a locomotive with a piece of thread. The power of man cannot prevent the purposes of God, although man is capable of abusing God's gifts, as we will see in Samson's life.

15. A FRESH JAWBONE OF A DONKEY: This jawbone was evidently from a donkey that had died fairly recently. The sun would have quickly dried out the bone, making it brittle and of little use as a weapon. Once again, we see Samson touching a dead body, directly against his Nazirite vow.

KILLED A THOUSAND MEN: Here we discover an incongruous fact: the Lord had placed Samson under a special set of regulations, including the provision that he not touch anything dead, and Samson persistently ignored those rules—yet the Lord, within His providential purposes, chose to use Samson (in spite of his sinful shortcomings) to perform miraculous feats against Israel's enemies just the same. Samson single-handedly stirred up the people of Israel to rise against the Philistine oppression. Nonetheless, that conflict would not be completed until the time of David.

SLAUGHTERING AN ARMY MAKES A MAN THIRSTY: *Samson finds himself thirsty and cries out to God. Yet his attitude reveals the strong hold that his physical desires have in his life.*

16. HEAPS UPON HEAPS: This is a pun, since the Hebrew word for *heap* is similar to the word for *donkey*. Samson was quite fond of puns and word play; see Judges 14 for the word game he played with his wedding guests—a game that led to disaster.

17. RAMATH LEHI: Literally, "hill of the jawbone."

18. NOW SHALL I DIE OF THIRST? : There is an almost petulant tone to this challenge, as though Samson were trying to threaten or bully God. He recognized that the great victory had come through the power of God, not through his own might, and he did not fail to give God the glory. Yet physical needs and desires were also a powerful motivating force in Samson's life, and the two forces were constantly at war within him. On his way to his wedding feast, he found a beehive full of honey and could not resist satisfying his physical appetite—despite the fact that the honey was inside the carcass of a dead lion. This struggle of flesh versus spirit plagued Samson for his entire life, and ultimately led to a tragic end.

19. GOD SPLIT THE HOLLOW PLACE: God's grace and mercy are abundantly evident in the life of Samson, as they are throughout all of Scripture. Samson's life was not characterized by faithful obedience, yet the Lord continually showed him grace and met his needs.

EN HAKKORE: Literally, "caller's spring," or, "spring of the one who cried out."

Samson Meets a Prostitute: Samson's flesh now leads him further down the path to destruction—yet the Lord still uses him to plague the Philistines.

1. Gaza: One of the five major Philistine cities, site of the modern city of Gaza. Each Philistine city had a standing army of its own, and they were the best-trained and best-equipped fighting forces in Canaan at the time.

saw a harlot: Samson's physical lusts were leading him down a course to ruin.

3. the doors of the gate of the city and the two gateposts: The city of Gaza was probably constructed with a double wall surrounding it, similar to Jericho (see Study 6). There would have been a high-vaulted passageway between the walls, with heavy gates set into the outer wall (and possibly another set of gates on the inner wall). These gates would have been constructed of very thick wood, reinforced with iron. The gates would be locked at night with a huge oaken beam set into iron brackets (the "bar" referred to here). The gate posts would have been set into the walls themselves, and the entire structure was designed to withstand a besieging army and its battering rams. There was simply no human possibility that one man could have ripped those gates out of the walls. Yet Samson ripped them down, then hoisted them onto his shoulders—a mass of architecture more than ten feet tall and weighing several tons—and carried them to the hill facing Hebron, a city that was some thirty-eight miles away—uphill!

Enter Delilah: *Samson's fleshly indulgences finally lead him into contact with Delilah, who works for the Philistines. It is also Samson's downfall.*

4. Delilah: Delilah was probably a Philistine herself; she was certainly not a Hebrew, and Samson had no business becoming involved with her. She is renowned in literature and art as a deadly seductress, but the fault of Samson's fate lay more with Samson than with her.

5. find out where his great strength lies: The world marveled at the superhuman feats Samson had performed, and evidently only Samson recognized that the power came directly from God. Yet, as we will see, even Samson did not fully comprehend these miracles, as he attributed God's indwelling to some mystical connection with his long hair—the one stipulation of his Nazirite vow that he did not disobey.

6. Please tell me where your great strength lies: Thus began the tragic downfall of Samson, as Delilah repeatedly questioned him and he repeatedly deceived her. It seems incredible that a man of his stature would fail to recognize that she was in the service of the Philistine lords, trying to seduce his secret for his own destruction. Yet Samson's life had not been characterized by wisdom; he had repeatedly violated the word of God and had used the Lord's great gifts for his own purposes. A lifetime of folly will lead one to ever greater folly, even to the point of self-destruction.

9. THE SECRET OF HIS STRENGTH WAS NOT KNOWN: The interesting thing is that the Lord never instructed Samson to keep his strength a secret, so far as we know. The Lord was filling Samson with His Holy Spirit specifically so that Samson might bring to God's people deliverance from the Philistines, and it would have been far more effective if Samson had publicly proclaimed that his great strength came directly from the Spirit of God. But as we have seen, he was more interested in using that gift to gratify his own desires.

16. HIS SOUL WAS VEXED TO DEATH: This sequence of seduction apparently continued for some period of time, perhaps over many months. Samson had placed himself in the power of the enemy by involving himself in an immoral relationship with Delilah, and this gave her the ability to nag him and goad him and seduce him until he finally couldn't stand to hear it any longer. His only hope was to repent of his sinful habits, abandon Delilah, and purify his life—but he failed to do that, and ultimately his spiritual strength wore out. His physical strength followed close behind.

17. THEN MY STRENGTH WILL LEAVE ME: There is no indication in Scripture that Samson's strength was directly tied to his long hair. Rather, his hair was an outward symbol of his own submission to the Spirit of God; in fact, it was the *only* outward symbol of submission, since he had violated all the other commandments of his Nazirite vow. The one element of Samson's statement that is accurate is his comment that he would "be like any other man" if his hair were cut, since it was the final act of rebellion against God's commands. By cutting his hair, Samson was openly declaring that he had fully rejected his calling—and at that moment, he became like any other man.

HE DID NOT KNOW THAT THE LORD HAD DEPARTED: *Samson makes his final choice to betray his Nazirite vows, and the Spirit of God leaves him. But not forever.*

20. HE DID NOT KNOW THAT THE LORD HAD DEPARTED FROM HIM: This is one of the saddest statements in Scripture. It indicates that Samson had taken the Lord's presence for granted and that he had no intimate relationship with the God of Israel—he was not even aware when God's Spirit had left.

21. PUT OUT HIS EYES: Samson had made himself spiritually blind by repudiating the Lord's commands, so now his enemies made him physically blind as well.

22. THE HAIR OF HIS HEAD BEGAN TO GROW AGAIN: This should not be construed to mean that, as Samson's hair grew, so did his miraculous physical strength. During his time in prison, Samson evidently had time to reflect upon his life and his divine calling, and his final prayer reveals that he had repented of his squandered life.

25. BETWEEN THE PILLARS: Archeologists have unearthed Philistine temples that were similar to the one in Gaza. They were constructed with two major pillars near the center, which bore most of the weight. The temple in Gaza evidently included an open courtyard surrounded by a multistoried temple. The lords and ladies watched Samson perform like a trained circus animal in the courtyard, comfortably seated in surrounding balconies.

28. SAMSON CALLED TO THE LORD: In this brief prayer, Samson referred to the Lord by three different biblical names: *Adonai*, *Yahweh*, and *Elohim*. This suggests that he had come to a fuller appreciation of God's character during his time of imprisonment, and had fully repented of his sins. Ironically, he needed to have his physical eyes gouged out before his spiritual eyes were opened. Samson had allowed his fleshly desires to take priority over his spiritual calling and had consequently been far less effective for God than he might have been otherwise. Nevertheless, he is listed among the great heroes of the Christian faith (Hebrews 11:32), another demonstration of the grace of the Lord.

∽ First Impressions ∽

1. How would you characterize the life of Samson? What were his great strengths? What were his great weaknesses?

2. Why did the Lord empower Samson to slaughter three thousand Philistines? Why did He enable him to tear the gates from Gaza? What was He working to accomplish?

3. *What was the "secret" of Samson's great strength? What does this teach you about God's involvement in the lives of His people?*

4. *Why did Samson tell Delilah how to enslave him? What led him to that point? Why did he not foresee what would happen?*

⤳ Some Key Principles ⤳

The Lord does not abandon us when we sin, but sin can ruin our lives.

It is somewhat surprising to read about the life of Samson, so plagued with fleshly indulgence, and to realize that the Spirit of God continued to use him in mighty ways. He appears to have spent much of his life consorting with the enemies of his people. He indulged in wine despite his Nazirite vow to refrain from it. He married a Canaanite woman, which was forbidden of God's people. He even hired prostitutes and carried on an immoral relationship with Delilah—yet the Lord used him to begin the overthrow of the Philistines. Samson's life is hardly an example for godly behavior, and yet he is listed among the heroes of the faith in Hebrews 11.

The sad fact is that Samson's effectiveness was greatly limited by his own sin and selfishness. Instead of being both a political leader and spiritual example in Israel, Samson was a moral failure who accomplished far less than his potential. Though Samson would make a dent in Philistine control over Israel, the Philistines would not be entirely defeated until a man appeared who had a whole heart for God—and that man was David. The Lord used Samson to accomplish a small part of His plan, but his sinful habits prevented him from accomplishing as much as he could have.

The Lord does not abandon His children when we sin, but our sinful habits can severely interfere with our effectiveness in His service. Our sin grieves the Holy Spirit and quenches His power in our lives. When we walk in ungodliness, we risk ending in tragedy, just as Samson did.

The Lord restores those who repent.

Samson lived his life indulging every desire of his flesh, with no apparent remorse. He squandered his great gift of strength in many ways, using it for personal revenge and to get himself out of scrapes that he had gotten himself into in the first place. He ignored his great calling to lead Israel out of bondage, and as far as we know he never made any attempt to lead the men of Judah into battle. He violated his Nazirite vows and flagrantly disobeyed many of the Lord's injunctions against immoral behavior.

Yet at the end of his life, he repented and turned back to the Lord—and the Lord used him in the mightiest and most dramatic accomplishment of all. Samson had tragically lost many opportunities to accomplish great deeds for the Lord, but that did not prevent the Lord from restoring him to service.

This is the good news that follows the bad news in our previous principle. Sin can damage a believer's life, and it can limit that person's effectiveness in God's service. But that does not mean that He has washed His hands of us—the Lord is always at work to bring us back into full fellowship with Him, making us fit vessels for His service. As long as we have the breath of life, we have the opportunity to make ourselves right with God. He will always restore those who genuinely repent of sin, and He will use us for His glory. "If we confess our sins, He is faithful and just to forgive us our sins and to cleanse us from all unrighteousness" (1 John 1:9).

Christians have the Spirit of God living within them.

Samson believed that his great strength came from some magical effect of never cutting his hair. He did not seem to understand that his power came from the Spirit of God, who had chosen to indwell him. When he unintentionally permitted Delilah to cut his hair, he was making a public statement repudiating his Nazirite vows—he was openly declaring that the God of Israel was not his Lord. His life was ruled instead by his own passions.

The same Holy Spirit who empowered Samson also indwells every Christian. The Holy Spirit, of course, is not an impersonal force. Rather, He is a divine Person, who as the third Member of the Trinity is coequal and consubstantial with the Father and the Son. The Bible teaches that the Spirit has all of the attributes of personality and deity, including intellect, emotions, volition, eternality, omnipresence, omniscience, omnipotence, and truthfulness. In the church age, which began on the Day of Pentecost recorded in Acts 2, the Spirit indwells believers, having regenerated them from sin and sealed them for future glory. The Spirit also sanctifies, instructs, illuminates, and empowers believers for spiritual service. He enables them to be obedient to the truth. When we walk in accord with the Word of God, which the Holy Spirit inspired, we walk according to the Spirit and thereby exhibit the fruit of the Spirit. On the flip side, when we gratify the desires of our sinful nature (as Samson did), we quench the Spirit and exhibit the fruit of the flesh (Galatians 5:16–25).

⤳ Digging Deeper ⤴

5. *Why did God continue to use Samson through so many years of disobedience? Why did the Spirit leave Samson when he cut his hair?*

6. *Why is Samson listed among the great heroes of the faith in Hebrews 11? What does this suggest about the grace of God?*

7. How do you think Samson's life might have been different if he had walked in godliness?

8. What principles of the conflict between flesh and spirit are illustrated in Samson's life? What principles of God's love are illustrated?

9. Is there an area of sin in your life that is hindering your walk with the Lord? What will you do about it this week?

10. How is the Spirit of God at work in your life at present? How will you submit yourself to His Word this week?

Section 3:

Themes

In This Section:

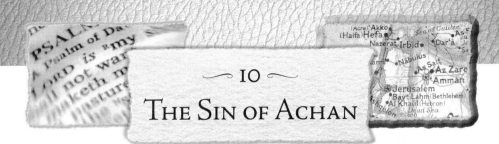

⤙ HISTORICAL BACKGROUND ⤚

We now return to the days following the battle of Jericho. The Lord had commanded the people to not take anything whatsoever away from Jericho after its fall—everything was to be destroyed as a sacrifice to God. The Lord had claimed the entire city of Jericho for Himself; it was to be His property, dedicated to Him and utterly set apart from the people.

But one man disregarded God's command, a man named Achan. Perhaps he convinced himself that God was speaking in broad, general terms—that He would not mind or even notice if one man took just a few small trinkets. Or perhaps he didn't think at all; maybe he just snatched what he saw without giving any thought to the possible consequences. Whatever he may have told himself, Achan fell prey to the sin of coveting, and it led to deadly consequences for his entire family.

In this study, we will look at Achan's story and consider the dangers of coveting. We will also see that we cannot hide anything from God, for He sees both what we do and what we think. This can be a sobering concept for us if we try to hide our sins from God, but it can also be a great deterrent from sin and temptation.

⤙ READING JOSHUA 7:1–26 ⤚

PREPARING FOR BATTLE: *Joshua prepares his army to attack Ai soon after the battle against Jericho. What he doesn't know, however, is that there is sin in the camp.*

1. THE ACCURSED THINGS: This passage took place after the fall of Jericho. The Lord had commanded the people to "abstain from the accursed things, lest you become accursed when you take of the accursed things, and make the camp of Israel a curse, and trouble it" (Joshua 6:18). God had condemned all of Jericho—all its inhabitants and all their possessions—to destruction, and the people were forbidden to carry away anything whatsoever. Achan, however, had taken a souvenir.

2. AI: See the map in the Introduction.

3. LET ABOUT TWO OR THREE THOUSAND MEN GO UP: This proved to be a gross strategic error and miscalculation. The spies thought that there were "few" inhabitants in Ai, yet it turned out that there were some twelve thousand people (Joshua 8:25)—far too many for a small force of three thousand, at least from a human perspective. The spies may have anticipated that the Lord would fight on their behalf, as He had done at Jericho and elsewhere; if so, their faith was commendable and was certainly justified later when the Lord did bring down Ai. In this case, however, there is no record that Joshua consulted the Lord prior to making his strategic plans. If he had, the Lord would certainly have told him to not attack at that time—there was sin in the camp that needed to be dealt with first.

ISRAEL'S FIRST DEFEAT: *As a result of Achan's sin, the Lord did not fight on behalf of His people. They found out what it was like to have God set His face against them.*

5. THE HEARTS OF THE PEOPLE MELTED: This is the phrase Rahab used to describe the dismay that the people of Jericho felt toward Israel. Because of Achan's sin, the Lord had removed His protective hand from His people, and they were experiencing the same dismay to which God's enemies were subject.

6. JOSHUA ... FELL TO THE EARTH ON HIS FACE BEFORE THE ARK OF THE LORD: Joshua's failure in this passage is that he had not done this in the first place, seeking the Lord's counsel before attacking Ai. He should have come before God and humbly sought His guidance before moving ahead.

9. WHAT WILL YOU DO FOR YOUR GREAT NAME?: Joshua's concern is twofold in his prayer: he is concerned for the welfare of the people for whom he is responsible; and he is worried that the Lord's name will be disgraced.

11. ISRAEL HAS SINNED: Here is a very important point in this passage: the Lord held the entire nation responsible for the sin of one man. Achan had hidden his sin, and it is unlikely that Joshua knew of it—yet Achan's family knew, and they had assisted him simply by keeping his secret. Thus, the sin of Achan had corrupted the entire assembly of God's people and was directly responsible for Israel's military defeat and the deaths of thirty-six soldiers.

12. THEY HAVE BECOME DOOMED TO DESTRUCTION: Note that, by taking an object that God had doomed to destruction, the people themselves also became doomed to destruction. Sin's consequences often go far beyond just the person sinning, affecting the lives of others. Such is the destructive power of disobedience.

Purging the Evil: *The Lord commands Joshua to find the guilty man and put him to death. The penalty extends to his family and all his possessions.*

15. burned with fire: This sounds like a dreadfully harsh punishment for such a "small" sin as looting a city that one's army had defeated in battle. But man's view of sin is often not harsh enough, for God detests sin and will not tolerate it in His presence. Furthermore, the Lord had warned that everything associated with Jericho was set aside for destruction, and anyone who took anything from the city would also bring destruction upon himself. Achan knew this beforehand but had deluded himself into thinking that he could deceive God.

19. give glory to the Lord . . . make confession to Him . . . tell me now what you have done: Achan had tried to hide his sin, and in doing so he had brought disgrace upon the Lord's name. By openly admitting his sin, he was glorifying God, acknowledging that he was guilty of breaking God's holy standard.

21. I saw: Note the four steps in Achan's sin: he *saw*; he *coveted*; he *took*; he *concealed*. David's sin with Bathsheba followed the same pattern (2 Samuel 11). "But each one is tempted when he is drawn away by his own desires and enticed. Then, when desire has conceived, it gives birth to sin," James tells us. But never forget the consequence: "Sin, when it is full-grown, brings forth death" (James 1:14–15).

24. all that he had: Once again, we are confronted with the fact that the sin of one man brought destruction upon many. His entire family was implicated because they each had assisted him in concealing the sin, and the Lord viewed that as being complicit in the sin itself.

⌁ First Impressions ⌁

1. *Why did the Lord command the Israelites to not take anything from Jericho?*

2. Why did Achan disobey the Lord's command concerning looting Jericho? What motivated him?

3. What was Joshua's main concern when Israel lost the battle against Ai? How did his attitude compare with Achan's attitude?

4. Why did Achan bury the loot under his tent? What did this reveal about his attitude toward God?

↬ SOME KEY PRINCIPLES ↫

The things of the world can bring corruption.

The army of Israel defeated Jericho, and it is customary for a victorious army to plunder the defeated foe. From the perspective of war, Achan was well within his rights to take a few things after the battle. The items he came away with were not evil in themselves—a beautiful garment, some cash, and a wedge of gold. The problem was that the Lord had clearly commanded His people to not take away *any* loot from Jericho. Interestingly, the Lord did permit the people to carry away loot from Ai. If Achan had simply obeyed at Jericho, he would have been more than compensated in the next battle.

The Lord frequently calls His people to refrain from worldly habits and pursuits—to obey His Word even when worldly pleasures tug our hearts in a different direction. The lust of the flesh, the lust of the eyes, and the boastful pride of life continually tempt us to sin. Like Achan, our hearts can be enticed by feelings of covetousness, greed, envy, and the desires of our flesh. The question is whether or not we will resist the temptation and be obedient to the Lord.

The principle here is that the Lord calls His people to be set apart from the world, and this frequently includes avoiding contact with worldly activities. "For you are the temple of the living God. As God has said: 'I will dwell in them and walk among them. I will be their god, and they shall be my people.' Therefore 'Come out from among them and be separate, says the Lord. Do not touch what is unclean, and I will receive you'" (2 Corinthians 6:16–17).

God cannot be deceived.

Achan understood the Lord's command to not touch any of the possessions in Jericho, but he believed he could take just a few small items without any consequences. He then buried those stolen items in the ground beneath his tent—an excellent hiding place if ever there was one. Achan and his family believed they could hide their sin from God.

The fact is, they did succeed in hiding their sin from other people. It would appear that nobody outside of Achan's family was aware of the stolen property, and Joshua confidently led the army into battle in the belief that all was well. But the Lord knew what Achan had done, and He was not willing to overlook the transgression. But all sin, no matter how small in the world's eyes, is an abhorrent offense in the eyes of God.

It is easy to hide our sins from the people around us, but we can never hide them from God. He calls His people to purify our lives from all sins and to confess them openly before Him. "Do not be deceived, God is not mocked; for whatever a man sows, that he will also reap. For he who sows to his flesh will of the flesh reap corruption, but he who sows to the Spirit will of the Spirit reap everlasting life" (Galatians 6:7–8).

Covetousness is the same as idolatry.

Achan was motivated by covetousness. He confessed that it was his own eyes that had led him into sin: he *saw* beautiful things in Jericho, and he coveted them in his heart. What he coveted, he also took; and what he took, he finally hid.

It is not a sin to admire beautiful things; it is a sin to *covet*. To covet is to lust for something, to fix one's mind on material possessions or financial gain. We begin to covet when we long to possess something that does not belong to us, when we become absorbed with getting what we don't have. Achan did not sin when he noticed that the garment in Jericho was lovely; he sinned when he determined that he had to own it, in spite of God's prohibition.

When we covet, we fix our hearts upon material goods, and those desires begin to drive our thoughts, actions, and attitudes. In this way, the thing we covet becomes like a god to us—an "idol" in our lives. The Lord wants us to fix our eyes on Him alone, turning them away from the goods of this world. "Put to death . . . covetousness, which is idolatry" (Colossians 3:5).

⤚ Digging Deeper ⤛

5.   *What were the steps in Achan's sin? When have you taken similar steps that led to sin?*

6. Why did God command that Achan's entire family be put to death? What does this severe punishment reveal about God's view of disobedience?

7. What exactly is covetousness? How is coveting an object different from admiring it? How can we tell the difference?

8. In what ways is covetousness the same as idolatry? How can we recognize it in our own lives?

9. Are you struggling with covetousness? What do you covet? What biblical principles and practical steps can you apply in your life to overcome this temptation?

10. Are you trying to hide any sins from God? If so, take time right now to confess those sins to the Lord. He is faithful and just to forgive (1 John 1:9).

THE KINSMAN REDEEMER

RUTH 4; GALATIANS 4

↬ HISTORICAL BACKGROUND ↫

Family and heritage were of paramount importance in Old Testament times. A man who had many sons considered himself blessed by God because his family line would increase and prosper through his offspring. Property was an inviolable heritage to a family; a piece of land that one inherited from one's father was to be kept in the family at all costs.

Therefore, it was a terrible tragedy to a man to die without a son, since the inheritance and family name were perpetuated through the male line. It meant that the family name would die out, and the ancestral property would go to someone else. In the eyes of the world at large, it was a sign of God's disfavor if a man died without an heir.

For this reason, the law made provision for a "kinsman redeemer," known as the levirate law. This stipulated that a close relative of the dead man could marry the widow on behalf of the deceased. Their firstborn son would take the name of the deceased, and he would inherit all of that man's property. In this way, the family line was continued, and the inheritance remained in the dead man's family.

As this story begins, all of Naomi's sons have died, and Ruth's late husband had not produced a son. They had already lost the family property through poverty, and the future looked very bleak for both women. Unless a close relative was willing to step up and marry Ruth, there was no hope for the family line.

Yet the Lord had it all under control. He had already planned to bring together Ruth and Boaz, as we saw in Study 5, and He worked out all the details through His divine sovereignty. In this study, we will consider the person of Boaz himself, looking at what he undertook when he became Ruth's kinsman redeemer. And in doing so, we will gain some better insight into the person and work of Jesus Christ.

⤙ READING RUTH 4:1–17 ⤚

SEEKING A REDEEMER: *Ruth's first husband is dead, and his family line will be permanently cut off—unless there is a relative willing to marry her.*

1. BOAZ WENT UP TO THE GATE: These events took place after the harvest was completed. Ruth had revealed her identity to Boaz, telling him that she was his close relative. He immediately determined to carry out his duty as kinsman redeemer—in this case, by marrying the widow of his near relation.

THE CLOSE RELATIVE OF WHOM BOAZ HAD SPOKEN: There was another man who was a closer relative than Boaz, and that man had the right to marry Ruth ahead of Boaz. The Hebrew word translated "close relative" refers to a person who acted as protector of the family rights. He could be called upon by family members to perform a number of duties: (1) to buy back property the family had sold; (2) to provide an heir for a deceased brother by marrying his widow (these two situations were facing Boaz); (3) to buy back a family member who had been sold into slavery due to poverty; (4) to avenge a relative's murder by killing the murderer. This is the same Hebrew word used of God as Redeemer in the book of Isaiah: "You shall know that I, the LORD, am your Savior and your Redeemer, the Mighty One of Jacob" (60:16). God is our "Close Relative," our "Kinsman Redeemer."

4. BUY IT BACK: Naomi's poverty had forced her to sell a piece of land that was part of her family inheritance. The people of Israel were not permitted to permanently sell family land, for the land itself ultimately belongs to the Lord. "The land shall not be sold permanently, for the land is Mine; for you are strangers and sojourners with Me" (Leviticus 25:23).

5. TO PERPETUATE THE NAME OF THE DEAD: In this somewhat complicated transaction, Boaz was telling his relative that he was obligated to do more than just purchase the land: he also would be obligated to marry Ruth if he took on the role of kinsman redeemer. The principle behind the kinsman redeemer was that a family line would die out if a man died without a son. The kinsman redeemer was to marry the widow and raise up a son who would carry on that family name. The firstborn son would receive the deceased man's inheritance, thus keeping property in the same family.

NOT WILLING TO PAY THE PRICE: *Being a kinsman redeemer was a costly undertaking. What's more, the cost was all for someone else's benefit.*

6. LEST I RUIN MY OWN INHERITANCE: This unnamed relative evidently was willing to purchase the family field, but not willing to marry Ruth. His reasons are not entirely clear, but it is possible that he was unwilling to buy the field only to have it pass on to a different family line. (The first son born to him and Ruth would bear the name of Ruth's first husband, rather than his.)

10. THAT THE NAME OF THE DEAD MAY NOT BE CUT OFF: The concept of being "cut off" was of profound importance to Israel. It meant to be cast out of the camp, to be deprived of access to God's presence. (Remember that the Lord's presence was visibly with the camp of Israel during their wilderness wanderings, prior to arriving in Canaan.) In a metaphorical sense, the name of Ruth's deceased husband would be similarly cut off, lost to all memory among God's people. This would be prevented, however, if Boaz married Ruth and raised a son in the dead man's name.

12. LIKE THE HOUSE OF PEREZ: The people at the gate blessed Boaz and Ruth, asking the Lord to make them fruitful with offspring. They mentioned Rachel and Leah as significant examples in Israel's history, since they were the wives of Jacob who bore most of his sons (the fathers of the twelve tribes of Israel). It is interesting that Perez was also singled out in this list, however, since he was technically an illegitimate son born of an incestuous union (Genesis 38). Yet the Lord's grace is demonstrated by the fact that Perez was in the line of Christ. Boaz was a descendant of Perez, and Boaz's descendants included David and Jesus.

14. WHO HAS NOT LEFT YOU THIS DAY WITHOUT A CLOSE RELATIVE: The Lord Himself had blessed Ruth by providing a "close relative" or redeemer in the person of Boaz. The Lord blesses all mankind in a far greater way by providing us with the true Redeemer, our greatest Close Relative, Jesus Christ.

15. WHO IS BETTER TO YOU THAN SEVEN SONS: Naomi had misunderstood the character of God previously, when she publicly proclaimed, "The hand of the LORD has gone out against me!" (Ruth 1:13). Now she saw for herself that God had never abandoned her or turned His back on her—quite the opposite, in fact. In the end, she was blessed far beyond the losses she had suffered, made more poignant by the fact that she nursed the grandfather of David.

17. OBED: Obed's son Jesse was the father of David. Jesus was descended through David's line.

⤳ READING GALATIANS 4:3–7 ⤳

JESUS IS OUR KINSMAN REDEEMER: *God used the experiences of Ruth and Boaz to paint a picture of His ultimate plan: to redeem mankind as His own inheritance.*

3. IN BONDAGE: The human race was in bondage to sin and death, "the elements of the world," and there was no hope of redemption prior to Christ. We had been "cut off" from God, and there was absolutely no possibility of being reinstated into God's grace.

4. BORN UNDER THE LAW: Boaz and the unnamed "close relative" present an important contrast. The unnamed man was unwilling to submit himself to the levirate law, unwilling to become Ruth's kinsman redeemer, because it would have cost him something. Boaz, on the other hand, willingly submitted to his responsibilities and became Ruth's kinsman redeemer. Jesus is the Creator of the universe, God the Son, the Word made flesh, the only human ever to live a sinless life—yet He willingly submitted Himself to becoming a man, born under the law, in order to redeem us. Being "under the law" includes the fact that Christ willingly allowed Himself to face temptation on our behalf— yet without sin—and He submitted to the ultimate curse of mankind by voluntarily dying on the cross.

5. TO REDEEM THOSE WHO WERE UNDER THE LAW: As those who had violated God's law, we had no hope of eternal life, no prospect of being reconciled to God: we were dead in our sins, and we were doomed to be eternally cut off from the Father. Yet God Himself provided the way: He became our Kinsman Redeemer, and through Christ we are no longer cut off but are redeemed into eternal life and fellowship with God.

ADOPTION AS SONS: When we receive Christ as our Redeemer, we are "born again" into the family of Jesus, and we inherit all that He owns—which is to say, all that there is in eternity. We receive the name of Christ, and we even develop His character—we come to look and act just like our Redeemer through the Holy Spirit's refining work.

6. ABBA, FATHER: "Abba" is a term of affection similar to our word *Daddy*. Through the Holy Spirit, we are able to cry out to God in a relationship that is very intimate— crying out to Him, "Daddy!" Christ's work of redemption takes us from being cut off and fatherless into a deep relationship of intimacy with our eternal Father.

7. YOU ARE NO LONGER A SLAVE BUT A SON: We are given, free of charge, an eternal inheritance and an everlasting family. Boaz redeemed Ruth's inheritance with gold, but Christ redeemed us with something infinitely more valuable: His own precious blood. "You were not redeemed with corruptible things, like silver or gold, from your aimless conduct received by tradition from your fathers, but with the precious blood of Christ, as of a lamb without blemish and without spot" (1 Peter 1:18–19).

↶ First Impressions ↷

1. If you had been in Boaz's place, how would you have responded when Ruth told you that you were her close relative?

2. If you had been in Ruth's place, how would you have responded to Boaz's actions? How would you have felt when the other man refused to become your redeemer?

3. Why did the other relative refuse to become Ruth's kinsman redeemer? Why did Boaz accept the responsibility? What do these responses reveal about the character of God?

4. What did it cost Boaz to become the kinsman redeemer? What did Ruth gain? What did Naomi gain?

↬ Some Key Principles ↫

Mankind has no hope apart from Christ.

Ruth's first husband had died without producing a son and heir. This meant that his family line would cease to exist, a terrible fate in Old Testament times, which suggested that God Himself had cut off that man's family. There was no hope of changing that situation either, since Ruth by herself could hardly produce a son in her husband's family line. The only solution was to have a relative of her dead husband marry her and produce a son in the late man's name—a situation that was completely out of Ruth's control.

The Bible makes it abundantly clear that the human race is cut off from God in its sinful, unredeemed condition. God detests sin and cannot permit it into His presence. Yet every descendant of Adam has sinned; we are born with a sinful nature, and nothing can ever remove it—"for all have sinned and fall short of the glory of God" (Romans 3:23). "All we like sheep have gone astray; we have turned, every one, to his own way; and the LORD has laid on Him the iniquity of us all" (Isaiah 53:6).

But God had planned from before the foundation of the world to redeem mankind to Himself. He knew that no descendant of Adam could redeem the fallen race, because every person born from Adam's line would inherit his nature—the *sin* nature. The only way mankind could be redeemed was through the Son of God, Jesus Christ who was born of a virgin. Jesus committed no sin, yet He died voluntarily on the cross, taking upon Himself the punishment due to Adam's sinful race.

Jesus is our Kinsman Redeemer.

Ruth was doomed to a life of poverty, bereft of property and kin. There was nothing she could do to change her circumstances, and her only hope lay in the hands of a stranger who had little to gain from a marriage to her. Yet Boaz rose voluntarily to the call of duty and took upon himself the full responsibility of caring for his relatives. What's more, he was in love with Ruth! He did not marry her in a grumbling spirit of obligation, but with a joyful, enthusiastic attitude.

Boaz provides us with a small picture of Christ in His role as our Redeemer. We were without hope, without inheritance, without a future, and there was nothing we could do to change that grim picture. Yet Jesus took upon Himself the full responsibility of caring for us, and He is preparing a place for us as His bride for all eternity. He did this voluntarily, not out of any compulsion—even to the point of willingly dying on the cross.

And best of all, He loves us! Jesus was willing to die on the cross because He yearned for our fellowship, longed to be reunited with His fallen creatures. He knows us intimately, even to numbering the very hairs of our heads, and He delights in our company. He is our joyful Redeemer, the One who bought us back with His own blood—and did so willingly.

Christ's redemption is free to us, but very costly to God.

The role of kinsman redeemer involved a heavy responsibility. It almost certainly included some financial burden, and could even put a man at risk of his own life. One of his responsibilities might be to see justice done for a murder, calling him to take the life of the murderer with his own hands. Boaz's relative was unwilling to pay the cost of redeeming Ruth because it would have a negative impact on his own inheritance. But Boaz did not hesitate to pay whatever cost was required because of his great love for Ruth.

Jesus knew even before He went to the cross that He would be called upon to pay the ultimate cost to become our Redeemer. Like Boaz, He was under no obligation to pay that cost, for He had never sinned. Nevertheless, He chose voluntarily to pay the full cost of His own sinless life, fulfilling the Redeemer's role of putting to death the enemy of mankind: death itself.

Ruth did nothing to attain the love and redemption of Boaz; he paid the full price, and she received it simply by saying, "I do." We, too, receive God's redemption freely, at no cost to ourselves: the price has been paid in full at the cross by Jesus Christ. By embracing Him in faith, we receive the priceless redemption of eternal life—a redemption that cost God the life of His only Son.

↪ DIGGING DEEPER ↩

5. *In what ways has Boaz's faithfulness influenced the world?*

6. *How do Boaz's actions as a kinsman redeemer point to the redemption of Christ?*

7. What does it mean that Jesus is our Kinsman Redeemer? What does that role entail?

8. Why did Jesus voluntarily become our Kinsman Redeemer? What did it cost Him? What did we gain?

ᔐ Taking It Personally ᔐ

9. Have you embraced Jesus Christ as your Redeemer and Lord? If not, what is preventing you?

10. If you have accepted Christ as your Savior, what does that mean long-term? What inheritance do you have? What guarantees do you have?

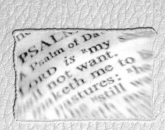

Section 4:

Summary

Notes and Prayer Requests

⌁ 12 ⌁
REVIEWING KEY PRINCIPLES

⌁ LOOKING BACK ⌁

We have covered a large span of time in Israel's history in the previous eleven studies, and we have met many memorable people along the way. The encouraging thing to recognize is that these were real people, and we have seen them just as they really were—blemishes and all. What's more, they were confronted by real life, sometimes facing life's more dramatic events, sometimes facing everyday routine. Many have proven faithful to God; some have not.

But one theme has remained constant throughout these studies: God is *always* faithful. Some of the characters we've met, such as Ruth, trusted Him implicitly; others, such as Samson, were prone to trust only themselves; yet God remained faithful to His word and to His people from beginning to end. If you come away with only one thought from these studies, let it be this: God is *always* faithful.

Here are a few of the major themes we have found. There are many more that we don't have room to reiterate, so take some time to review the earlier studies—or better still, to meditate upon the passages of Scripture we have covered. Ask the Holy Spirit to give you wisdom and insight into His Word. He will not refuse.

⌁ SOME KEY PRINCIPLES ⌁

God can literally move heaven and earth to accomplish His purposes.

Or, to speak more accurately, the Lord will cause the earth and heavens (the atmosphere) to *not* move. In order for the sun to "stand still," the earth itself would need to stop revolving on its axis—and this evidently is exactly what the Lord did for the Israelites one momentous day. He literally caused the earth to stop for a period of hours simply so that His people might have victory in battle.

The Lord went beyond even this "earthshaking" miracle when He moved heaven itself—the abode of God—to send His Son to earth as a man. He temporarily set aside the laws of biology, causing a virgin to become pregnant with the Son of God. More than this, He permitted His Holy One to take on the sin of mankind; He caused the One who is Life to taste death; He subjected the Creator to the whims of those He had created. And He did all this so that we might be reconciled with Himself.

If God was willing to do all of this for the sake of sinful people in the past, He will certainly prove faithful in meeting your present needs. Some problems may be too great for your power to resolve, but there is no problem too great for God. He will move heaven and earth to show Himself faithful to His people.

Do not be afraid, but be strong and of good courage.

This commandment appears frequently in the book of Joshua—usually at times when there seemed to be genuine cause for fear. Prior to one battle, the army of Israel had marched all night long, uphill, carrying all their gear for battle. They had arrived to face not one but five enemy armies, and they were already tired before the battle even began. Yet the Lord commanded His people to not give in to fear.

Fear is the enemy of God's people. It moves us away from faith, and toward disobedience. The people of Israel arrived at the Jordan River, ready to take possession of the promised land, but their spies brought back a discouraging report: there were giants in the land, and fortified cities! The people yielded to fear and disobeyed the Lord. As a result, that entire generation was doomed to die in the wilderness without entering the promised land (Numbers 13–14).

We are commanded to resist fear, which demonstrates that fear is something that we can master. This is done by shifting our focus away from the situation that threatens us and focusing on the Lord who redeems us. He is absolutely sovereign over all our affairs, and He is completely faithful to save His people. If He was willing to make the sun stand still for Israel's army, He will be willing to intervene in your life as well.

Do not fall into a cycle of sin and repentance.

The people of Israel had disobeyed the Lord's command to drive out the Canaanites, and this led them into idolatry and immorality. The Lord responded by sending hardship upon them as a form of discipline, urging them to return to obedience and purity. The oppression of enemies and other calamities forced Israel to repent and return to the Lord, and He graciously sent judges to lead them back to obedience. But after a time, the people lost interest in the things of God and soon began the cycle all over again.

This cycle was not pleasing to God. He wants His people to obey Him willingly, to worship Him voluntarily, with whole hearts. God will send discipline into the lives of His children to make us purer and more like Christ, but His desire is that we obey Him out of love and gratitude, rather than by the compulsion of hardship. It is a mark of spiritual maturity to obey God's Word simply because we know that it pleases and glorifies the Father.

Christians are to obey God's commands, not to negotiate for a "better deal."

Barak was the leader of Israel's military, and as such he was probably accustomed to having his commands obeyed without argument. After all, a good soldier never talks back to a commanding officer; he carries out the commands without comment. It was all the more startling, therefore, when Barak countermanded the direct orders of his Commanding Officer—God Himself.

Picture a general commanding a soldier to move into battle, and the soldier responds, "I will go into battle only if you come with me; if you will not come with me, I won't go." That soldier's career would be short. Yet how much more audacious is it when a believer tries to find ways around simple obedience to God's Word! We do this when we obey only partway, or tell ourselves that we will begin to obey tomorrow, or when we ignore the promptings of the Holy Spirit.

The Lord wants His people to obey His Word with willing hearts—not by compulsion. We cannot experience the Lord's full blessing in our lives unless we willingly obey His commands. As Deborah sang, "When the people willingly offer themselves, bless the LORD!" (Judges 5:2).

Ask God for guidance, but don't put Him to the test.

The Scriptures abound with men and women who were faced with difficult circumstances or decisions, and they turned to the Lord for guidance. Jesus urged His disciples to seek the Father's will in all things, teaching them to pray, "Your will be done on earth as it is in heaven" (Matthew 6:10). Today, Christians receive the indwelling of the Holy Spirit, whose role in part is to guide us into all truth (John 16:13). There is no excuse for putting God to the test in order to receive direction.

Of course, this was not what Gideon was really doing when he put out his fleeces. The Lord had *already* given him guidance, telling him exactly what he was to do—but Gideon was afraid. He feared that the Lord would not keep His promises, so he sought miraculous verification of God's faithfulness. The Lord had repeatedly proven Himself faithful throughout Israel's history—parting the Jordan River for them to cross, bringing down the walls of Jericho, giving His people one victory after another against powerful enemies—and Gideon should have rested in faith that the Lord would keep His word once again.

Modern Christians also have a record of God's faithfulness through the ages. We learn of it throughout the Bible, as we read the testimonies of those who have walked with Him in the past. If we live in light of God's Word, obeying the truth He has revealed to us in Scripture, we can do so with confidence—knowing that God will be faithful in the present just as He has been in the past.

God cannot be deceived.

Achan understood the Lord's command to not touch any of the possessions in Jericho, but he believed he could take just a few small items without any consequences. He then buried those stolen items in the ground beneath his tent—an excellent hiding place if ever there was one. Achan and his family actually believed they could hide their sin from God.

The fact is, they did succeed in hiding their sin from other people. It would appear that nobody outside of Achan's family was aware of the stolen property, and Joshua confidently led the army into battle in the belief that all was well. But the Lord knew what Achan had done, and He was not willing to overlook the transgression. But all sin, no matter how small in the world's eyes, is an abhorrent offense in the eyes of God.

It is easy to hide our sins from the people around us, but we can never hide them from God. He calls His people to purify our lives from every sin and to confess them openly before Him. "Do not be deceived, God is not mocked; for whatever a man sows, that he will also reap. For he who sows to his flesh will of the flesh reap corruption, but he who sows to the Spirit will of the Spirit reap everlasting life" (Galatians 6:7–8).

Covetousness is the same as idolatry.

Achan was motivated by covetousness. He confessed that it was his own eyes that led him into sin: he *saw* beautiful things in Jericho, and he coveted them in his heart. What he coveted, he also took; and what he took, he finally hid.

It is not a sin to admire beautiful things; it is a sin to *covet*. To covet is to lust for something, to fix one's mind on material possessions or financial gain. We begin to covet when we long to possess something that does not belong to us, or become absorbed with getting what we don't have. Achan did not sin when he noticed that the garment in Jericho was lovely; he sinned when he determined that he had to own it, in spite of God's prohibitions.

When we covet, we fix our hearts upon material goods, and those desires begin to drive our thoughts, actions, and attitudes. In this way, the thing we covet becomes like a god to us—an "idol" in our lives. The Lord wants us to fix our eyes on Him alone, turning them away from the goods of this world. "Put to death . . . covetousness, which is idolatry," the apostle Paul wrote (Colossians 3:5).

Jesus is our Kinsman Redeemer.

Ruth was doomed to a life of poverty, bereft of property and kin. There was nothing she could do to change her circumstances, and her only hope lay in the hands of a stranger who had little to gain from a marriage to her. Yet Boaz rose voluntarily to the call of duty and took upon himself the full responsibility of caring for his relatives. What's more, he was in love with Ruth! He did not marry her in a grumbling spirit of obligation, but with a joyful, enthusiastic attitude.

Boaz provides us with a small picture of Christ in His role as our Redeemer. We were without hope, without inheritance, without a future, and there was nothing we could do to change that grim picture. Yet Jesus took upon Himself the full responsibility of caring for us, and He is preparing a place for us as His bride for all eternity. He did this voluntarily, not out of any compulsion—even to the point of willingly dying on the cross.

And best of all, He loves us! Jesus was willing to die on the cross because He yearned for our fellowship, longed to be reunited with His fallen creatures. He knows us intimately, even to numbering the very hairs of our heads, and He delights in our company. He is our joyful Redeemer, the One who bought us back with His own blood—and freely chose to do so.

↳ DIGGING DEEPER ↲

1. *What are some of the more important things you have learned from the books of Joshua, Judges, and Ruth?*

2. Which of the concepts or principles have you found most encouraging? Which have been most challenging?

3. What aspects of "walking with God" are you already doing in your life? Which areas need strengthening?

4. Which of the characters we've studied have you appreciated or identified with the most? How might you emulate that person in your own life?

5. Have you taken a definite stand for Jesus Christ? Have you accepted His free gift of salvation? If not, what is preventing you?

6. In what areas of your life have you been most convicted during this study? What exact things will you do to address these convictions? Be specific.

7. What have you learned about the character of God during this study? How has this insight affected your worship or prayer life?

8. List below the specific things you want to see God do in your life in the coming month. List also the things you intend to change in your own life in that time. Return to this list in one month and hold yourself accountable to fulfill these things.

If you would like to continue in your study of the Old Testament, read the next title in this series, *Prophets, Priests, and Kings*, or the previous title, *The Exodus from Egypt*.